FOR OUR TWO ANGELS

Who taught us to live with a generous spirit, eat well and laugh often.

•

CONCETTA MAZZITELLI DI FLORIO
KONSTANTINOS YOTIS

ANTHONY YOTIS
LAURA DI FLORIO YOTIS

THE FISHMONGER'S SON

THE EXPERT GUIDE TO BUYING, PREPARING & COOKING SEAFOOD

plum. Pan Macmillan Australia

CONTENTS

INTRODUCTION

Thank you for picking up this cookbook. We are Anthony and Laura, the husband-and-wife team behind The Fishmonger's Son, a neighbourhood fishmonger in Melbourne's Carlton North.

Seafood is a natural part of our life, our celebrations and our everyday cooking. Talking to our customers, it struck us that this is not so for many; while Australians love seafood, they are often hesitant about cooking it at home. And that's really why we wanted to write this book: to encourage readers to branch out beyond their comfort zone (often salmon fillets and prawns!) and explore the incredible variety and quality of seafood we have access to in Australia. It is so simple to cook and prepare at home, and the flavour possibilities are endless.

We have included step-by-step instructions for the basics, like shucking oysters and peeling prawns, as well as our recommendations for the best seafood for curries, barbecuing, crumbing and more. We have also included a simple home cook's guide to the most popular seafood – how to select the best piece, what to expect in terms of flavour and texture, and what dishes it works best with.

But first, a quick history of how we got here.

*

Anthony was born into a seafood family. For 40 years, his father, Kon, and his uncle, Tim, drew a loyal following at the Footscray Wholesale Market, priding themselves on supplying high-quality, fresh fish to Melbourne retailers. Anthony worked as a fishmonger alongside his dad for many years, venturing out and exploring different trades, but always returning to the family business. He dreamed of one day owning his own seafood shop, and that dream became something we began to work towards together.

When we finally landed on what the shop would be, it was obvious that it would be called The Fishmonger's Son as a tribute to Anthony's father, who passed away in 2014. It would also be deeply connected to our respective Greek and Italian cultures; we coined the term 'seafood deli' as a nod to the continental delis of our childhoods. We wanted to redefine what a fishmonger was. We wanted to showcase all types of seafood, so many of which are more often found in a delicatessen than a fishmonger. Anchovies and other smoked, pickled and canned fish sourced locally and from around the world were high on our list.

The stars aligned in 2018, when we opened our shop and hit the ground running – the Carlton North community warmly embraced us and our little family, and it's been home ever since. We recently relocated the shop to a larger space further up the road, which has renewed our energy and set the stage for the next part of our seafood journey.

As well as celebrating beautiful fresh fish from Australia and New Zealand and specialty seafood from around the world, we wanted our shop to be an unpretentious space where shoppers can pick up all the ingredients to create a great seafood meal for a midweek dinner or a special occasion. Besides our mainstays and seasonal specialities, Anthony always ensures our display has fresh-cut marinara mix, a fish for baking, one for a stew or curry, a good sashimi option or two and a nice fish to pan-fry.

We have always agreed that we will only stock items in the shop that we have personally tried and love, and we have used the same approach for this cookbook. Many of the recipes in this book are inspired by how we cook at home, how we celebrate and entertain with seafood. There are treasured family recipes we have grown up with, such as Laura's mum's Tuna Risotto with Tomato & Olives (page 120) and Anthony's family favourite, Avgolemono Fish Soup (page 195), and others that have come from talking to our customers and learning how they cook at home, such as the Ocean Trout Almondine (page 152). There are mainstays we sell in-store, such as our famed Prawn & Cray Roll (page 86) and The Fishmonger's Son Fish Pie (page 160), and comforting dishes we like to make for our family, such as Blue-eye Parcel with XO Sauce (page 142) and Seafood Youvetsi (page 196). Like our shop, this cookbook reflects who we are, our passion for eating well and simply, and our mission to encourage customers and readers alike to try something new.

We hope this book encourages you to embrace seafood in all its incarnations. Whether you buy your fish and seafood from a fishmonger, a market or a supermarket, this book is for you.

We have brought together a collection of simple family recipes that we hope will inspire you to broaden your horizons and see how easy it is to incorporate seafood into your everyday life.

Thank you for coming along on this journey with us,

A&LX

TFS

SEAFOOD GUIDE

FAVOURITE FISH

FOR THE HOME COOK

This is by no means an exhaustive list of all things seafood. It comprises readily available species that are easily found at your local fishmonger or market. In our store, we have found salmon, flathead and rock ling are consistently the most popular fish being purchased.

BARRAMUNDI

Barramundi is a quintessential Australian species, available wild (when in season between February and November) or, more commonly, farmed. Barramundi imported from Asia can also be found (it will usually have been frozen), but it is preferable to buy sustainably farmed barramundi. When raw, it is a light grey colour. Ensure it is not slimy as this indicates it's not fresh.

Barramundi is low in fat and a good source of omega-3s.

FLAVOUR & TEXTURE

Barramundi is a mild, white fish with a fluffy texture when cooked. It is wonderful to pan-fry skin-side down. Be mindful not to overcook it, as it can get quite tough.

BEST COOKING

Use barramundi whole or filleted. It is great with Asian flavours – think ginger and lemongrass. It will steam beautifully, or really elevate a curry (see page 154). It makes wonderful fish cakes (see page 176), but works just as well pan-fried with a crispy skin.

PAIR WITH

Asian flavours

Stir-fry noodles

SUBSTITUTE

Blue-eye, ling, snapper

SASHIMI

Barramundi can be eaten raw but ensure you buy sashimi-grade fish.

BLUE-EYE TREVALLA

Anthony's favourite! Blue-eye trevalla is available year-round and is caught wild, coming in from New South Wales down to South Australia, or imported from New Zealand. A medium-sized fish weighing in at 2–5 kg whole, it makes nice-sized fillets (great for cooking for a few people) or steaks. When purchasing this from your fishmonger or market, look out for an even-toned, whitish flesh; if it's looking a bit pink or 'stained', it may not be super fresh. It should not have a distinct odour.

FLAVOUR & TEXTURE

Blue-eye has a mild flavour and firm, white flesh with a large flake once cooked. It's delicious!

BEST COOKING

Use whole, filleted or as cutlets.
Lovely to bake en papillote (see pages 142, 151 and 154), pan-fried or barbecued. It also makes a beautiful soup.

PAIR WITH

A simple side of warmed greens and a good squeeze of lemon

Asian flavours, crispy chilli oil and steamed rice

SUBSTITUTE

Bass grouper, hāpuku, trumpeter

SASHIMI

Exquisite eaten raw, but check with your fishmonger to ensure it is sashimi-grade.

FLATHEAD

Flathead is a true Aussie icon. Once a bycatch, it is the second-most popular fish we sell in our store and is available Australia-wide year-round, with an abundance from July through to September on the eastern seaboard. There are many different species, including tiger, dusky and rock. A good fishmonger will amend the price depending on supply and quality. Look for a fresh pink colour and gloss; if the fillets look dull and slimy or have any odour they are not fresh. Rock flathead is our fave if you ever come across it; it has a lovely greyish flesh and a milder flavour than the pink-fleshed varieties.

FLAVOUR & TEXTURE

Flathead has a soft texture with fine flakes and a distinct flavour. Compared to other, oilier fish, it is dry, so be sure not to overcook it.

BEST COOKING

You can cook flathead whole or as fillets. Flathead fillets lend themselves well to being cooked quickly, crumbed, battered or floured with the skin off. It is also a lovely fish to bake whole. If you buy a whole fish, keep the bones for fish stock.

PAIR WITH

Classic seafood pairings such as citrus, tartare and salads

Fresh panzanella salad (see page 170)

SUBSTITUTE

Other flathead species, whiting

SASHIMI

Exquisite eaten raw, but check with your fishmonger to ensure it is sashimi-grade.

GARFISH

Available for most of the year, garfish is a small, slender fish with a pencil-like beak and a silvery sheen. There are several species of garfish, the most commonly available being the southern garfish. As kids we would eat these floured and fried. Buying them butterflied is convenient as they have many fine bones when eaten whole. They are lovely to cook whole, with a flaky skin, and the spine is easy to remove, coming out in one piece.

FLAVOUR & TEXTURE

Garfish has sweet, delicate, white flesh.

BEST COOKING

Garfish can be prepared whole, butterflied or filleted. It's great to grill or pan-fry with an edible skin. Some people like to barbecue them whole. We love them floured and shallow-fried in some good olive oil.

PAIR WITH

Classic seafood flavours such as citrus

Fresh herbs

SUBSTITUTE

Snapper, whiting

SASHIMI

Exquisite eaten raw, but check with your fishmonger to ensure it is sashimi-grade.

HOW TO SKIN A FISH FILLET

Place the fillet skin-side down on a cutting board. We find it much easier to skin the fillet if the board and the fillet have a little water on them; this helps the knife to glide smoothly.

If it's a long fillet with a pointy end, grab it from the tail end. If it's a portion, you will notice a separation at the belly side where you should insert and rest your knife.

Use your fingers to hold the tail or belly piece and slide your knife in flat, with the blade tilted slightly towards the board.

Slide the knife in one single motion, separating the skin from the flesh, so you are left holding the skin with your fingertips.

KINGFISH

Kingfish is available wild-caught year-round in Australia and sustainably farmed in South Australia, where it is referred to by its Japanese name, hiramasa. The farmed variety generally has a higher fat content and a firmer, more consistent texture. A whole fish can range in size from 3–10 kg, with the farmed species mostly in the 3–5 kg range.

Kingfish is an excellent source of omega-3s.

FLAVOUR & TEXTURE

Kingfish has firm, white flesh with a slightly oily texture and unique flavour. The skin is not edible.

BEST COOKING

You can grill or barbecue kingfish, but treat it as you would a fine steak and do not overcook it. It's lovely for a curry due to its firm texture. If using fillets, leave the skin on when cooking. Remove the skin if serving raw. If baking or grilling, we suggest en papillote.

PAIR WITH

Citrus, capers and olive oil for a European take on crudo

Wasabi and soy for a Japanese vibe

SUBSTITUTE

Marlin, swordfish, tuna

SASHIMI

Yellowtail kingfish is excellent eaten raw as carpaccio (see page 81), crudo or ceviche and highly prized for sashimi.

MACKEREL

Blue or slimy mackerel is a small, oily, wild-caught fish that can be found around the Australian coast. It's much smaller than other mackerels, with the average size being 300–700 g, although they do grow larger.

It is high in omega-3s and very well priced.

FLAVOUR & TEXTURE

Blue or slimy mackerel is a firm, oily fish with a strong flavour. The flesh is reddish brown and the skin is thin and edible.

BEST COOKING

Use mackerel whole, butterflied or filleted. It can be barbecued, fried, baked, poached, grilled and cured. When cooked whole, we suggest scoring the thickest part of the fish. It is particularly good hot smoked.

PAIR WITH

Strong flavours such as citrus, tomato or 'nduja

SUBSTITUTE

Bonito, sardines or other mackerel varieties

SASHIMI

Mackerel is suitable for sashimi, often cured first.

THE BEST FISH FOR SASHIMI

Select a fish that is sashimi-grade and has a nice texture. As well as those below, you can also use sashimi-grade blue-eye, calamari, King George whiting, scallops, snapper and swordfish – check with your fishmonger.

ATLANTIC SALMON

KINGFISH

TUNA

KING SALMON

HOW TO CUT SALMON SASHIMI

This is optional, but we like to neatly trim the ends of the fillet first.

You will see a white bone line in the centre of the fillet.

Run a very sharp knife along either side of the bone line and discard the piece with the bone line. You should now have two pieces of fish.

Technique is most important here – you don't want to drag the knife. You should slice in a straight, single motion to create each sashimi slice about 2–3 mm thick.

OCEAN TROUT

Trout was introduced to Australia via the Americas. Ocean trout and rainbow trout are the same species, the difference being one has been raised in saltwater and the other in freshwater, respectively. Farmed at sea and growing to 3–5 kg, ocean trout is available year-round and has become an Australian staple.

Trout is high in omega-3s.

FLAVOUR & TEXTURE

Trout has a more subtle and delicate texture and flavour than salmon. It has a firm, deep orange flesh.

BEST COOKING

Use trout whole, filleted or as cutlets. It can be baked, poached and pan-fried. It's also wonderful smoked or cured. We recommend cooking it with the skin on, although the skin is generally not eaten.

PAIR WITH

Classic fresh flavours such as citrus, dill and crème fraîche

SUBSTITUTE

Atlantic salmon or king salmon

SASHIMI

Lovely for sashimi, with a delicate, slight oiliness – always buy sashimi-grade.

RAINBOW TROUT

Rainbow trout and ocean trout are the same species, the difference being one is raised in freshwater and the other in saltwater, respectively. Rainbow trout is farmed sustainably in land-based tanks or waterways and is generally available year-round. Grown to 'plate size', they are wonderful to bake whole in the oven.

FLAVOUR & TEXTURE

Rainbow trout have a delicate, soft, pink flesh with a small flake.

BEST COOKING

Cook whole, butterflied or filleted. It's good for baking and poaching and wonderful smoked, cured or made into a pâté (see page 58), or tossed through a pasta.

Leave the skin on when cooking – it will peel away easily when serving. Be mindful of the bones, they are fine and plentiful.

PAIR WITH

Citrus

Crème fraîche

Olives

SUBSTITUTE

Ocean trout, salmon

SASHIMI

Ocean trout is a better sashimi option.

ROCK LING

This a very versatile, wild-caught, white fish that has been a staple at Australian tables for many years. It is available nearly year-round, coming in from Australian and New Zealand waters. The most common varieties of ling are rock ling and pink ling. Buy ling skinned and filleted. A chunky fillet is perfect for a curry.

FLAVOUR & TEXTURE

Rock ling has a mild flavour. It's not an oily fish. When comparing it to seafood from other parts of the world, it is most like an Atlantic cod.

BEST COOKING

Fillets are best cooked with the skin removed. It is good for curries (see pages 154 and 209) and stews, as well as crumbed and fried. It's also suitable for smoking and perfect as an addition to fish pie (see page 160).

PAIR WITH

Curry

SUBSTITUTE

Hāpuku, monkfish

SASHIMI

Not suitable to be eaten as sashimi.

SALMON

Salmon is by far the most popular fish sold in Australia. It significantly out-sells everything else, despite the controversy surrounding farmed salmon. Atlantic salmon is commonly farmed in Tasmania, while king salmon comes from New Zealand.

Salmon is rich in protein, low in saturated fats and high in omega-3 fatty acids.

FLAVOUR & TEXTURE

An oily and rich-tasting fish, salmon has orange flesh and a distinct flake once cooked.

BEST COOKING

Salmon can be prepared whole, filleted or as cutlets. It's a very versatile fish that is great for baking, pan-frying, curing and smoking.

PAIR WITH

Asian flavours

Dill and lemon

SUBSTITUTE

Ocean trout

SASHIMI

Atlantic salmon is perfect for for eating raw, but if you're looking for something richer, king salmon makes for melt-in-the-mouth sashimi due to its higher fat content. Either way, ensure you buy sashimi-grade salmon.

SNAPPER

Snapper is a wild-caught species and a favourite all round. There are many varieties of snapper available, including pink, goldband, red, saddletail and ruby; all are equally delicious. Pink snapper is commonly available year-round. Both fillets and whole fish are available, with whole fish weighing in at 500 g up to a few kilograms.

FLAVOUR & TEXTURE

Snapper has soft, white flesh once cooked, with a sweet, mild flavour.

BEST COOKING

Prepare snapper whole or as cutlets or fillets with edible skin. It's lovely to bake, pan-fry, steam, poach or barbecue. When cooked whole, we suggest scoring the thickest part of the fish.

It also makes a beautiful soup, such as avgolemono (see page 195).

PAIR WITH

Citrus

Fresh herbs

SUBSTITUTE

Blue-eye, red emperor and other varieties of snapper

SASHIMI

Snapper is lovely eaten as sashimi, but check with your fishmonger to ensure it is sashimi-grade.

SWORDFISH

Also known as broadbill, swordfish is generally available year-round. Australian swordfish is second-to-none, coming in from the east coast. Fillets are taken from the loin. The flesh is a lovely, translucent pale pink that cooks to a bright white. It can handle a higher heat than most fish, making it ideal to cook on the barbecue.

FLAVOUR & TEXTURE

Swordfish has a mild flavour, and a dense texture similar to good-quality meat.

BEST COOKING

Prepare the loin or fillets on the bone. The skin is not edible. It's a great fish for the barbecue (see page 92) or pan-fried (see page 188). Swordfish is not an overly oily fish, so be sure not to overcook it or it will dry out.

PAIR WITH

Capers, lemon and butter

SUBSTITUTE

Marlin, tuna

SASHIMI

Swordfish is highly revered as sashimi, but check with your fishmonger to ensure it is sashimi-grade.

TUNA

Tuna is a robust, streamlined fish with a deep red flesh in the winter and a lighter red in the summer months. They can reach hundreds of kilograms in weight and are highly prized. Yellow fin tuna is most commonly available in Australia, although in the winter months we see more blue fin tuna, which is at its prime in the colder months. Tuna can be used in many ways. Yellow and blue fin are great for sashimi, while albacore is a good cost-effective option for cooking with.

FLAVOUR & TEXTURE

Tuna has firm, dark flesh that looks like red meat. It has a distinct flavour.

BEST COOKING

Use cutlets or fillets. Eaten raw as sashimi or tartare (see page 82), tuna is a real delight. It's also lovely seared to medium, or even grilled – if overcooked it will dry out.

PAIR WITH

Soy and wasabi if eating raw

With a traditional niçoise salad (see page 187)

SUBSTITUTE

Other species of tuna (albacore, big-eye, yellow fin and blue fin), marlin, swordfish

SASHIMI

Incredible eaten as sashimi, especially the belly (otoro), which is highly regarded in Japanese culture, but be sure to buy sashimi-grade.

SHELLFISH & MORE

FOR THE HOME COOK

In this section, we take you through shellfish basics, including how to clean mussels and peel prawns. We demystify calamari and octopus and give you a crash course on establishing your own seafood pantry.

CALAMARI

Squid is often referred to as calamari (an Italian word for squid) here in Australia. While there are many varieties, southern calamari is the most widely available. Squid has tentacles and ink, which is released as a defence mechanism. The ink is also a delicacy and is wonderful when used to make pasta.

FLAVOUR & TEXTURE

Calamari has firm, white flesh with a mild yet easily identifiable flavour.

BEST COOKING

Calamari is versatile: it can be fried, barbecued, stuffed and stewed. It's delicious simply floured and flash-fried.

PAIR WITH

A simple, fresh salad

Works well with classic seafood pairings such as citrus and tartare

SUBSTITUTE

Arrow squid, cuttlefish, octopus

SASHIMI

Calamari makes lovely sashimi when expertly prepared.

CLAMS, PIPIS & VONGOLE

Clams, pipis and vongole are a type of bivalve mollusc. They usually have a white to light-coloured shell with different markings depending on variety and where they come from. Hand-harvested from sand beds, you need to ensure they are well rinsed and purged before cooking. Ask your fishmonger if they have been purged.

Clams, pipis and vongole are generally available year-round. They should be consumed the same day, but if you need to store them, keep them covered with a damp cloth in the warmest part of your fridge.

FLAVOUR & TEXTURE

Clams, pipis and vongole have a firm texture and a subtle flavour and aroma of the sea. The flesh is a pale beige colour that firms up as it cooks.

BEST COOKING

Cook in the shell, but ensure they are well rinsed first. Discard any shells that don't open when cooking. They are lovely to pan-fry, steam or poach. We especially enjoy pasta vongole (see page 116).

PAIR WITH

Classic pasta dishes, such as pasta vongole

Stir-fried with Asian flavours

SUBSTITUTE

Clams, pipis and vongole can be used interchangeably

SASHIMI

Definitely suitable for sashimi, but always check with your fishmonger to ensure they are sashimi-grade.

CRAB

The most common species of crab we see through the market are blue swimmer, mud crabs, sand crabs and spanner crabs. They vary significantly in size and appearance, with the blue swimmer probably the most readily available – it is wild-caught and found around most of the Australian coastline. When buying, look for weight, vibrant colour, intact shells and claws – crabs should have a fresh oceanic aroma.

FLAVOUR & TEXTURE

Crab has soft, sweet, white flesh.

BEST COOKING

Whole or picked crab meat is wonderful and can be purchased raw or cooked. Crab can be steamed, poached, wok-tossed and fried. We adore a good crab pasta (see page 115).

PAIR WITH

Asian flavours

Chilli

Omelette

Pasta

SUBSTITUTE

Lobster, Moreton Bay bugs

SASHIMI

Not suitable.

CRAYFISH

The rock lobster is affectionately known as a 'crayfish' in Australia and is a real luxury. Wild-caught and strictly managed by quota, there are four main species hailing from different parts of the continent: southern rock, eastern rock, tropical and western rock lobster. It's ideal to purchase crayfish live, but many people prefer to buy cooked lobsters or raw frozen cray tails. Look for intact limbs, no discolouration and a fresh aroma of the sea.

FLAVOUR & TEXTURE

The flesh is translucent when raw and bright white when cooked. Crayfish has a sweet, rich flavour with a just-firm flesh.

BEST COOKING

Use the crayfish whole or just the tail. You can steam, poach or barbecue crayfish until the shell is bright orange-red.

PAIR WITH

Classic seafood flavours such as citrus

Good-quality mayonnaise and mustard (see page 86 for our prawn and cray roll)

SUBSTITUTE

Bugs, crab, prawns and other varieties of crayfish

SASHIMI

Crayfish makes exquisite sashimi, but it must be expertly prepared from live.

MORETON BAY BUGS

Closely related to crayfish, Moreton Bay bugs are something of a delicacy. They are wild-caught predominantly in New South Wales. They are most often available frozen, but you may find them fresh in limited supply. They grow to 10–15 cm long and have a broad, flat head, light brownish red shell and five pairs of small legs.

FLAVOUR & TEXTURE

Moreton Bay bugs have firm flesh that is mild and delicately sweet in flavour.

BEST COOKING

It is best to buy bugs raw. They can be cut in half and steamed, barbecued or poached.

PAIR WITH

Classic seafood pairings such as lemon, olive oil and fresh aromatic herbs

Mayonnaise

SUBSTITUTE

Balmain bugs, lobster, yabby

SASHIMI

Can be suitable for sashimi, but always check with your fishmonger to ensure it is sashimi-grade.

MUSSELS

The blue mussel – a bivalve mollusc – is an underrated treasure. They are cheap, farmed sustainably, readily available year-round, full of nutrients and easy to prepare. When buying, you should notice a distinct sea aroma; if they are no good they will smell bad immediately or once cooked. If you are preparing them in the shell, see the instructions on page 40.

FLAVOUR & TEXTURE
Mussels are moist with a distinct, oceanic flavour and a just-firm texture when prepared correctly.

BEST COOKING
Cook them in the shell by steaming or poaching in a pot. They can also be barbecued, smoked and pickled. Do not overcook mussels: once the shells open, remove from the heat to stop them getting tough and chewy.

PAIR WITH
Pasta or good bread

White wine, tomato, saffron, fresh herbs

SUBSTITUTE
Clams, pipis, vongole

SASHIMI
Can be suitable for sashimi, but always check with your fishmonger to ensure it is sashimi-grade.

HOW TO CLEAN MUSSELS

Ideally buy and cook mussels on the same day. If you need to store them, remove from any packaging and cover with a damp towel in the fridge. Be sure to discard any open mussels before preparing.

Rinse the mussels under cold water and remove any surface dirt.

Fill the sink or a large bowl with cold water and submerge the mussels.

Scrub the mussels with a steel wool scrub or stiff brush to remove any dirt and hairy bits.

Grasp the hairy 'beard', which will be sitting between the shells, and pull it out.

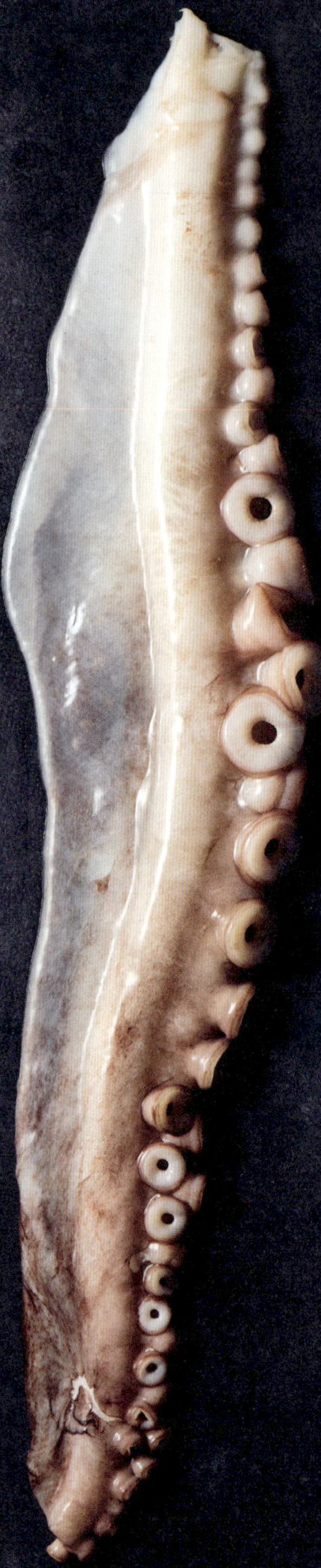

OCTOPUS

Octopus are cephalopods, like calamari and cuttlefish, and can be found around Australia. Some of the best octopus comes from Western Australia, where they are often found in cray pots preying on lobster. Octopus needs to be tenderised. If bought frozen it will usually already have been tenderised; if not, it should be 'beaten' or boiled and marinated to soften the flesh. Much like calamari, octopus lends itself to being cooked very quickly at high temperature or stewed very slowly.

FLAVOUR & TEXTURE

Octopus has a firm, dense texture – if overcooked it will be chewy. It is translucent when raw and bright white when cooked.

BEST COOKING

Octopus is great for barbecuing (see page 136), frying, braising and pickling (see page 61).

PAIR WITH

Classic European flavours such as citrus, tomato and olive oil

SUBSTITUTE

Baby octopus, calamari, cuttlefish

SASHIMI

Suitable for sashimi, but ensure it is expertly prepared.

OYSTERS

Oysters are somewhat of a luxury these days, sold by the dozen or half-dozen and often individually in restaurants. As estuarian bivalves, they are farmed sustainably in the waters of New South Wales, Victoria, Tasmania and South Australia. There are two main varieties of oysters available: the Sydney rock oyster, which is endemic to Australia, and the Pacific oyster.

Available year-round, oysters are at their peak in the cooler months. The rock oyster is generally smaller than the Pacific, with a slight yellow ring on the inner shell. The Pacific is plumper with a bright, beige flesh. In recent years we have seen the return of the native angasi oyster, which is like a French belon oyster.

FLAVOUR & TEXTURE

Shucked oysters should be plump and moist with an aroma of the sea. Live oysters should be closed, or should close when squeezed if they are slightly open. Rock oysters are small and have a saltier, briny flavour. Pacific oysters are plumper and have a creamier texture.

BEST COOKING

Oysters are best eaten raw, but can be steamed, grilled, barbecued, pickled and smoked.

PAIR WITH

A good squeeze of lemon

Asian-inspired dressings

Classic Kilpatrick

Mignonette dressing

SUBSTITUTE

Other oyster species

SASHIMI

Perfect for a sashimi platter.

HOW TO SHUCK OYSTERS

Starting with a folded kitchen towel and a shucking knife, place the oyster flat-side up on the towel. Use your dominant hand to hold the shucking knife. Feel your way around the outer rim of the oyster with the tip of the knife, looking for an entry point to break into the oyster.

Keep the oyster on the towel to hold the oyster steady and protect your hand in case of a slip. When you find the entry, work your way around the shell until you can lift the flat part of the shell – the oyster will be attached here.

Slide the knife under the oyster flesh between the suction point and shell to release the oyster. Discard the flat shell, leaving the oyster sitting in the curved part of the shell.

Give the oyster a slight rinse, if required, to remove any bits of shell. The better you get at shucking oysters, the less need for rinsing.

Use the knife to gently flip the oyster over in the curved part of the shell.

Now the oyster is belly-side up and ready to serve.

PRAWNS

As Australians, we do love a prawn. Prawn production is highly managed, with sustainable farming operations throughout southern, northern and north-eastern waters. Most prawns are harvested and processed out at sea. There are many species of prawn, including the popular king prawn, large tiger prawn, banana prawn, the Cape Moreton scarlet prawn and school prawns.

When buying, look for bright tails and translucent but firm shells. There should be no discoloration at the base of the head or legs and they should have a crisp, clean aroma.

Available in many sizes, prawns are classified in an old-fashioned way. U10s are the most common – U10 refers to ten per pound (or 22 prawns per kilogram).

FLAVOUR & TEXTURE

Prawns have an umami-rich, translucent flesh when raw and a bright, white, firm texture when cooked.

BEST COOKING

Cook whole or as cutlets. They are good poached, grilled and barbecued. Their firm texture works well in soup or a curry. Do not overcook them or they will become tough.

PAIR WITH

Citrus

Fresh herbs

Lemongrass

SUBSTITUTE

Bugs, crayfish and other species of prawn

SASHIMI

Suitable for sashimi

SCALLOPS

Scallops are bottom-dwelling saltwater bivalves nestled in fan-shaped, hinged shells. They are available farmed and wild-caught. There are a few varieties available in Australia, including Bass Strait scallops, which are commercially fished, the wild-caught ballot scallop and hand-dived varieties like the purple queen scallop. Scallops are usually sold as scallop meat or on the half shell. Look for translucent flesh and a dry quality, indicating they have not been frozen or stored in water.

FLAVOUR & TEXTURE

Scallops are rich with a slightly chewy texture.

BEST COOKING

Cook scallops quickly over medium heat; if overcooked they will be tough. They are wonderful pan-fried, grilled on the shell and barbecued.

See our recipe for a classic scallop pasta on page 112.

PAIR WITH

Aromatics

Butter

Citrus

SUBSTITUTE

Nothing really compares to a scallops, but texturally, mussels can work as a substitute

SASHIMI

Exquisite as sashimi, but be sure to seek out sashimi-grade scallops.

HOW TO PEEL PRAWNS

Hold the head of the prawn between your thumb and index finger.

Twist and pull the head, separating it from the body. You could also use a knife to cut the head off where the head ends and body starts.

From underneath the belly, between the legs, lift the shell and peel it back around the body, removing the legs and shell in one motion.

Peel off any remaining legs.

Run a small, sharp knife down the back of the prawn.

Use the tip of the knife to carefully remove the poop line. Now you have a prawn cutlet!

PRESERVED SEAFOOD

When we think about seafood, we don't just think about fresh fish, and neither should you! Preserved seafood has a good shelf life, is perfect for quick meals and an excellent addition for impromptu entertaining (see pages 60–67). Think of these as seafood pantry essentials.

SALMON CAVIAR
MOJAMA OF TUNA
BOQUERONES
(WHITE ANCHOVIES)
CAVIAR
SAN GREGORIO DE
POLANCO
OSCIETRA GRAND RESERVE
RIO NEGRO URUGUAY
BLACK CAVIAR
DESDE
1891
CONSERVAS
ORTIZ
El Velero
NET WT.
47,5g
ANCHOVIES in olive oil
ANCHOVIES

SEAFOOD ⚓ RECIPES

SNACKS & ENTERTAINING

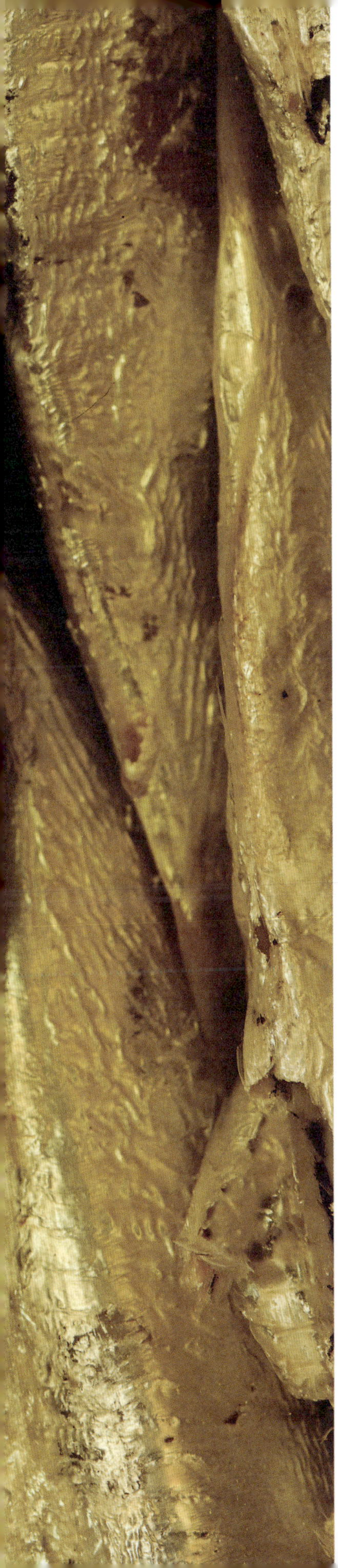

TARAMASALATA

A Greek national treasure. This dip is so easy to make, I'm not sure why we all buy it so often! Once you have mastered it, you'll never go back to store-bought. Our son Kosti eats 'tarama' sandwiches for his school lunch every day. If you want to fancy this dip up for guests, see the recipe on page 61.

MAKES 600 G

- 100 g white unsliced bread with the crusts removed (good-quality bread like Vienna or pasta dura – nothing too dense), left out for 1–2 days to stale
- 100 g tarama fish roe (see Notes)
- ½ small red onion, grated
- juice of 1–2 lemons
- 350 ml good-quality extra-virgin olive oil (see Notes), plus extra for drizzling

First things first, roughly tear up the bread and place it in a bowl of water to soak. Once the water has been absorbed into the bread, squeeze out as much water as you can and place the bread in the bowl of a food processor.

Add the fish roe and onion and blend to a smooth consistency. Now add half of the lemon juice and blend to combine.

Next, we want to create the magic ... time to add the extra-virgin olive oil to emulsify the ingredients. Using the food processor on slow–medium speed, slowly drizzle in the olive oil. You want to see the oil blend in to create a smooth, creamy texture.

It's time to taste! If it needs a bit more lemon or oil, now is the time to add it. The roe can be quite salty, so if you find it too salty add more bread. Blitz for another 5 minutes on high and add a tablespoon of water if needed to make it creamy.

We love to serve this with some toasted pita or crusty bread on the side and a drizzle of olive oil on top.

The taramasalata will keep in an airtight container in the fridge for 5–7 days.

NOTES We use and recommend Beach Gold Tarama, or if you have access to a good Greek deli the white tarama will be perfect. Depending on the roe you use, the colour of your taramasalata will vary from beige to light pink.

If your oil is too 'green' or 'young' it will impart a bitterness – we recommend using a Spanish, Greek or Italian oil from aged trees.

TROUT PÂTÉ

WITH CRÈME FRAÎCHE, LEMON ZEST & DILL

This trout pâté is something we pull together for spur of the moment catch-ups. It is quick to prepare and makes a wonderful addition to a grazing platter served with crostini. If you have time, make it the day before to allow the flavours to come together.

MAKES 400–500 G

- 250 g crème fraîche (see Notes)
- 100 g smoked trout fillet, flaked (see Notes)
- handful of dill fronds, finely chopped, plus extra to serve
- 2 spring onions, finely chopped
- salt flakes and freshly ground black pepper
- extra-virgin olive oil for drizzling
- zest of 1 lemon
- crostini (or bagel crisps or Melba toasts), to serve

Place the crème fraîche in a bowl. Add the trout, dill and spring onions and fold gently to combine. Add a little salt and pepper to season and a drizzle of olive oil. Add the lemon zest, then taste – you want enough zest to elevate the flavours without overpowering them.

Transfer to a serving bowl, cover, and pop into the fridge for 30–60 minutes to firm and allow the flavours to merge.

Serve with crostini on the side or dollop a little pâté on each crostini and present them to your guests on a tray, topped with a little extra dill.

The pâté will keep in an airtight container in the fridge for 2 days.

NOTES If you can't find crème fraîche you can use 250 g cream cheese.

You could just as easily substitute hot smoked salmon for the trout.

DRESSED-UP SEAFOOD

These are a few of our go-to dishes when friends are coming around. They're perfect additions to grazing plates or to serve as luxe appetisers. Best of all, these recipes are easy to pull together with store-bought items.

PICKLED OCTOPUS

Readily available from delis and fishmongers, moreish pickled octopus is further elevated by the addition of fresh aromatics. Very little effort for delicious gain!

250 g pickled octopus
2 spring onions, finely chopped
1 small red chilli, deseeded and finely chopped (substitute capsicum here if you don't like the heat)
2 tablespoons chopped flat-leaf parsley leaves
½ lemon, cleaned and segmented, skin and pith discarded – keep the flesh only
extra-virgin olive oil for drizzling

Heap the pickled octopus into a mixing bowl with enough room to stir through the additional ingredients. Put a little of the spring onion, chilli and parsley aside to sprinkle on top. Add the remaining spring onion, chilli, parsley and the lemon to the bowl and stir through. Transfer to a serving bowl and garnish with the remaining ingredients. Drizzle with olive oil.

MAKES 280 G

SMOKED SALMON
WITH LEMON ZEST & CAPERS

Many moons ago, Laura worked for one of Melbourne's leading art dealers, and this was a dish that was regularly prepared for staff and clients alike. It's one that we now often serve when we have friends around. The lemon zest really elevates the delicacy of the smoked salmon, while the capers are wonderful salty pops of flavour and the olive oil adds depth and richness.

100–200 g best-quality smoked salmon (we sell and love The Melbourne Pantry brand), cut into small pieces
50 g red onion, very finely diced
finely grated zest of 1 lemon
50 g small, salted capers, soaked and rinsed
extra-virgin olive oil for drizzling
salt flakes

Arrange the smoked salmon on a plate and scatter over the red onion, lemon zest and capers. Drizzle with olive oil, sprinkle with some salt flakes and enjoy with some crusty bread.

MAKES 250 G

TARAMASALATA
WITH SALMON ROE

The salmon roe and olive oil drizzle really elevate those iconic sea flavours of 'tarama', taking it from simple to luxurious in a flash.

200 g taramasalata (you can use a shop-bought one here or make your own, see page 56)
50 g salmon roe
extra-virgin olive oil for drizzling
finely grated zest of ½ lemon

Heap the taramasalata into a bowl and spoon the salmon roe on top. Drizzle with some olive oil and add a sprinkle of lemon zest. Serve immediately with fresh bread or good crackers.

MAKES 300 G

FRESHLY SHUCKED
OYSTERS WITH MIGNONETTE

We love to sit around the table and share a glass of wine at Easter or Christmas, while Anthony or my brother shuck oysters. This classic mignonette is a lovely contrast to the salty and briny texture of the oysters.

1 dozen (or 2 dozen!) Pacific or rock oysters, shucked
lemon wedges
finger lime caviar
salmon roe
black caviar

MIGNONETTE DRESSING

3 tablespoons finely diced shallots
125 ml (½ cup) champagne or rose vinegar
½ teaspoon coarsely ground black pepper
sea salt (optional)

In a glass jar, combine the shallot, vinegar, pepper and a pinch of salt. Taste as you go and adjust the balance. Pop the lid on and store in the fridge for at least 2 hours to allow the flavours to infuse before serving.

The dressing lasts for several weeks in the fridge, but the trick is to add your shallots 2 hours before ready to use, to ensure a vibrant and crisp flavour.

Arrange the freshly shucked oysters on a platter lined with some rock salt or ice, with the dressing on the side.

SERVES 6

TARAMASALATA WITH SALMON ROE

SMOKED SALMON WITH
LEMON ZEST & CAPERS
PICKLED OCTOPUS
FRESHLY SHUCKED
OYSTERS WITH MIGNONETTE

COOKED PRAWN CUTLETS
WITH EXTRA-VIRGIN OLIVE OIL & LOTS OF LEMON

We love to add a bowl of these to a summer grazing table. The lemon and olive oil pair so beautifully with prawns. (If you have time to peel your own prawns, they will be even better!)

500 g cooked prawn cutlets, tails on
2 lemons, 1 juiced and 1 cut into quarters
extra-virgin olive oil for drizzling
salt flakes, to serve

Arrange the prawns in a shallow dish. Dress these just before you're ready to serve them by adding the lemon juice and a good splash of olive oil. Sprinkle with salt flakes and arrange the quartered lemon on the dish. These will disappear in a flash!

SERVES 4 AS AN APPETISER

ANCHOVIES
& CRUSTY BREAD

Really high-quality anchovies are special, and when paired with great bread their simplicity and salty perfection is beautifully amplified.

48 g can premium anchovies (such as Ortiz, Olasagasti, Don Bocarte or Rizzoli)
1 small baguette

Slice the baguette into 1 cm rounds and place on a platter with the anchovies in the can on the side. Add small forks for serving. This is a lovely addition to a grazing table.

SERVES 4 AS AN APPETISER

CRÈME FRAÎCHE
& BLACK CAVIAR

When we do tastings in the store, this one is always well received. It's a lovely light starter on arrival when you have guests round.

pita crackers
200 g best-quality crème fraîche
10 g can best-quality black caviar

Arrange the pita crackers on a flat plate, spoon crème fraîche onto the crackers, then dollop a little caviar on each one. Ready to serve.

SERVES 6 AS AN APPETISER

PRAWN
& CRAYFISH APPETISERS

A nice if luxe alternative to a humble dip, for a Saturday afternoon snack or as an appetiser for guests.

This is the filling we use in our rolls (see page 86); if we're entertaining, we will keep a little aside, heap it into a bowl and serve with some fresh crusty baguette or little lettuce cups.

MAKES 300–400 G

COOKED PRAWN CUTLETS
WITH EXTRA-VIRGIN OLIVE
OIL & LOTS OF LEMON
PRAWN & CRAYFISH
APPETISERS

ANCHOVIES &
CRUSTY BREAD
CRÈME FRAÎCHE
& BLACK CAVIAR

EGG & MAYO DIP

WITH BLACK CAVIAR

Another family staple that has stood the test of time, this egg dip has made an appearance at nearly every Yotis family party since the 80s. It's moreish and nostalgic and even better the next day in a sando.

MAKES 630 G

- 1 small brown onion, finely grated
- 6 eggs, hard-boiled, cooled and mashed
- 3 tablespoons good-quality mayonnaise
- salt flakes and freshly ground black pepper
- 100 g black lumpfish caviar (see Notes)
- 1 packet Savoy biscuits

Combine the onion and egg in a bowl with the mayonnaise and season to taste. Add more mayo if you need to – the texture should be creamy (but not sloppy). Once you are happy with the flavour, spoon the dip into a small shallow serving bowl, creating a dome. Cover with plastic wrap and pop in the fridge for an hour.

Just before you are ready to serve, spread the caviar over the top. You want to completely cover the egg dome. Add some Savoys on the side and you are ready to serve.

The dip will keep in an airtight container in the fridge for 2 days.

NOTES You can pick up black lumpfish caviar at your local supermarket, but if you want to elevate this dish you can go all out with a beautiful black caviar.

Double the ingredients to scale this up for a crowd.

QUICK TUNA DIP

WITH CRUDITÉ PLATTER

This simple dip is a crowd-pleaser and a regular at many a family party. It's especially good accompanied with a crudité platter, but crackers or crusty bread will do just as well. It's also divine as a sandwich filling.

MAKES 500 G

celery leaves, to serve

TUNA DIP

2 × 185 g cans tuna in oil, drained
250 g cream cheese
1 celery stalk, finely chopped
1 small red chilli, finely chopped (optional – depending on your heat tolerance)
1 tablespoon double cream (optional; see Note)
salt flakes and freshly ground black pepper

CRUDITÉ

1 bunch of baby carrots (or small carrots, peeled and sliced in half)
1 pack baby cucumbers, quartered lengthways
1–2 celery stalks, cut into small batons
3–4 baby capsicums, quartered lengthways
1 bunch of baby radishes, halved

Place the tuna dip ingredients in the bowl of a food processor and process until well blended. Season to taste. Transfer to a bowl, cover with plastic wrap and refrigerate for at least 30 minutes to firm up. The chilli will add just a little heat, but you can always leave this out if you don't like spice.

In the meantime, prepare your crudité and arrange on a large platter, leaving space for the bowl of tuna dip.

Top the tuna dip with the celery leaves and place on the platter with the crudité.

The dip will keep in an airtight container in the fridge for 2 days.

NOTE Double cream adds a richness and creaminess to the dip.

THE BEST FISH FOR GRAVLAX

This traditional curing method usually uses salmon, with a mix of sugar, salt and dill.

ATLANTIC SALMON

KING SALMON

OCEAN TROUT

SALMON GRAVLAX

Another treasured family recipe that shines during the festive season, salmon gravlax is perfect for Boxing Day festivities – after we've recovered from the epic eating marathon that is Christmas Day.

SERVES A CROWD

400 g coarse or flaked sea salt, to cure

1 bunch of dill fronds, finely chopped

1 side Atlantic salmon (1 kg), pin-boned with skin on, halved

DRESSING

2 tablespoons finely chopped dill

2 tablespoons finely chopped flat-leaf parsley

1 teaspoon white sugar

2 teaspoons extra-virgin olive oil

2 teaspoons wholegrain mustard

125 ml (½ cup) white wine vinegar

salt flakes and freshly ground black pepper, to taste

Combine the salt and dill, then sprinkle evenly over the flesh side of each salmon half. Place the halves flesh to flesh, wrap tightly in foil and place in a shallow tray. This will catch any of the water that is released during the curing process, which you can then dispose of.

At this stage add a weight – for example, a brick wrapped in foil – to create some pressure to aid the curing process. Ideally you want the fish to cure in the fridge for 48 hours, rotating and draining it every 12 hours.

At around the 24-hour mark, it's time to make a jar of dressing (see Note) that can be tucked away in the fridge until you're ready to serve. Combine all your dressing elements in a jar and give it a good shake. Set aside in the fridge for all the flavours to merge and infuse.

Once the salmon is ready, unwrap it and brush off the salt and dill mixture. Finely slice the salmon and lay the pieces on a platter. Drizzle the dressing on top of the salmon. (We often serve extra dressing on the side for those wanting a little more.) Ensure you have some artisan bread to enjoy it with.

The smoked salmon will keep in the fridge for up to 4 days – perfect for those lazy post-Christmas days.

NOTE The dressing recipe will yield around 250 ml.

THE BEST FISH FOR CEVICHE

Choose a firm white fish with a light flavour for ceviche.

KINGFISH

SNAPPER

BLUE-EYE
HĀPUKU

KINGFISH CARPACCIO

This is a lovely way to eat raw fish and a definite crowd-pleaser. Carpaccio is super simple to prepare and it really lets the kingfish shine. In the warmer months when we have friends over, we love to serve this as a starter paired with a glass of bubbles or a crisp white.

SERVES 4 AS AN APPETISER

400 g piece kingfish, skin off, thinly sliced (2–3 mm thick) (see Notes)

juice of 1 lemon

2 tablespoons extra-virgin olive oil

1 tablespoon red peppercorns, roughly crushed

flaked seaweed salt, to serve (see Notes)

1 lemon, sliced and cut into small segments, skin off

Arrange the kingfish on a serving dish, being careful not to overlap the slices. Cover with plastic wrap and pop in the fridge until almost ready to serve (you can prepare up to 1 hour ahead).

Once your guests have arrived, take the kingfish out and let it sit for 10–15 minutes at room temperature.

Carefully drizzle the lemon juice over each piece; this will commence the process of curing. Follow up with the olive oil and finish off with the peppercorns and salt, then arrange the small lemon segments over the kingfish and serve immediately.

NOTES Ask your fishmonger to skin the kingfish and remove any blood line.

If you can't find seaweed salt, a good-quality flaked salt will work just as well.

TUNA TARTARE

GUACAMOLE

When we close for the week late on a Saturday afternoon, we like to make guacamole and hang out with the kids on the back deck with some wine and get into weekend mode. This guacamole-meets-tuna-tartare comes from this little family ritual of ours and is a lovely appetiser.

SERVES 4–6 AS AN APPETISER

500 g sashimi-grade tuna
2 tablespoons extra-virgin olive oil
juice of 3–4 limes
½ red onion, finely chopped (or chunkier if you prefer)
4 avocados
salt flakes and freshly ground black pepper
chilli oil
250 g bag corn chips or tortilla chips
handful of coriander leaves, to serve

Cut the tuna into 1 cm cubes and place them in a large stainless-steel mixing bowl. Add the olive oil, half the lime juice and the red onion. Give it a good mix to make sure the tuna pieces are coated, then set aside while you prepare the avocados.

Peel and cut the avocados into 1 cm cubes, then place them in a separate bowl. Use a fork to mash lightly. Add the rest of the lime juice, some salt flakes and freshly ground black pepper to taste.

Add the avocado mix to the tuna bowl and stir gently to combine. Add chilli oil and taste. Adjust the heat to your palate – you can add more lime and salt here too, if needed.

Once you're happy with the flavours, decant all of it into a shallow bowl in a nice little pile and pop it into the fridge for around 15 minutes. The flavours improve once it sits for a while.

Prepare a large round platter with your bowl in the middle surrounded by the chips. Top the guacamole with the coriander leaves and dig in!

SANDWICHES
WRAPS & MORE

PRAWN & CRAY ROLL

We were chuffed that our humble little roll was named as one of the best lobster rolls by Urban List. Our roll was born of a desire to create a takeaway offering in early 2020. We started with a prawn roll and decided it needed a bit more oomph ... enter the cray. This delicious little roll rose to fame during the infamous Melbourne lockdowns and has since become a signature of our store.

MAKES 4

24 cooked prawn cutlets, tails off, chopped into 1 cm pieces

200 g cooked crayfish meat, chopped

handful of finely chopped spring onion (or chives work well here too)

a good handful of finely chopped flat-leaf parsley leaves

1½ cups Japanese mayonnaise

zest and juice of 1 lemon

1 tablespoon Dijon mustard

4 banh mi dinner-size rolls

4 gem lettuce leaves, washed and trimmed

½ red onion, finely sliced, to serve

freshly ground black pepper

In a bowl, combine the chopped prawns, crayfish, spring onion, parsley and 1 cup of the mayonnaise, then add the lemon zest to taste. You want to taste all the elements and ensure they are well coated with mayonnaise. We like it quite lemony, but adjust to your taste.

In another bowl, mix the Dijon mustard and the remaining mayonnaise. Add a teaspoon or so of lemon juice so it's well balanced and not too strong.

Next, cut your rolls in half ready for the filling.

Spread the Dijon mayo on the bottom of the roll. Lay a leaf of gem lettuce on top. Spoon on the prawn and crayfish mix. Garnish with a few fine rings of red onion and a sprinkle of black pepper.

Ready to serve!

LOVE
IS IN THE

CRISPY-SKINNED SNAPPER BAO

We first fell in love with bao on our trips to Hong Kong, where we used to visit the wonderful Little Bao, run by chef May Chow. You can put almost anything in a bao, including prawns or crumbed fish. This version is with crispy-skinned snapper.

MAKES 12

1 × quantity seasoned flour – see Master Recipe for Floured Fried Seafood (page 165)
6 small snapper fillets (600 g total), skin on, cut in half lengthways
½ Lebanese cucumber
2 spring onions, green parts only
125 ml (½ cup) olive oil
12 bao buns
hoisin sauce, to serve
Japanese mayonnaise, to serve
sesame seeds, to serve

Place the seasoned flour in a deep bowl. Coat all of the snapper pieces and set them aside on some baking paper.

Peel and slice the cucumber and spring onion into thin batons, the length of the bao. Gather the rest of the ingredients together so that you are ready to assemble everything when it's time.

Heat the olive oil in a frying pan over medium heat. Fry the snapper pieces in batches until crispy and golden, about 2 minutes each side. While the snapper is frying, steam the bao buns according to the packet instructions.

Open the bao and layer the hoisin, cucumber, spring onion and snapper. Add another drizzle of hoisin, then the mayonnaise, then sprinkle some sesame seeds on top. Be generous here so you get a good flavour combo.

We also love to place all the components on a large board or platter in the middle of the table and have everyone assemble their own.

SMOKED SALMON & CAVIAR SANDWICHES

We love this classic combo for an afternoon tea spread! It features at so many of our family gatherings with 'the aunties' and reminds us of these treasured times together. The sandwiches are super simple to put together – it's really all about the layering and colour – and they taste pretty yummy too!

MAKES 16 TRIANGLES

8 slices of soft, square white bread
250 g cream cheese, softened
50 g black lumpfish caviar (see Note)
200 g smoked salmon, finely sliced

Spread the cream cheese evenly over each slice of bread, not too thick, but ensure you cover the whole piece.

Next, thinly spread the caviar on four slices of the bread and lay slices of smoked salmon on top.

Now you can put the sandwiches together, cut the crusts off and cut into triangles.

Arrange on a pretty platter to serve.

NOTE You can pick up black lumpfish caviar at your local supermarket, but if you want to elevate this dish you can go all out with a beautiful black caviar.

BARBECUED SWORDFISH SOUVLAKI

When we first moved in together we used to make chicken souvlaki as a nod to Anthony's Greek heritage. Over the years we've experimented with different proteins and this swordfish version is currently our fave. Souvlakis are just so delicious and simple to prepare.

MAKES 4 GENEROUS SKEWERS

6 short bamboo skewers
600 g swordfish, skin off
2 tablespoons extra-virgin olive oil
½ teaspoon lemon zest
salt flakes and freshly ground black pepper
1 lemon, cut in half
4 pita breads
4 tablespoons labne (or strained yoghurt)
¼ iceberg lettuce, chopped
1 tomato, chopped
½ red onion, finely sliced

Start by soaking the skewers in a bowl of water for at least 30 minutes (this prevents them from burning). You can just as easily use metal skewers if you have them.

Warm your barbecue or a griddle pan on medium heat.

Prepare the swordfish by cutting out the blood line and cutting into 2 cm cubes. (You can always ask your fishmonger to remove the blood line.)

Place the swordfish pieces in a bowl with the olive oil, lemon zest and salt and pepper to taste. Combine to coat the fish.

Assemble the skewers by threading the swordfish on. Pop them onto the heat and cook for around 2–3 minutes each side. The flesh will turn a bright white as it cooks through. You want to achieve a nice smoky charred flavour and golden colour.

Once cooked, set the skewers aside and generously squeeze lemon over the swordfish.

Add the pita to the same hot plate to char a little on both sides.

Once all your elements are ready it's time to assemble ... pita, labne, lettuce, tomato, swordfish, then onion and season to taste. Fold them or roll them up and enjoy. You can also arrange the elements on a board or large platter and assemble at the table as you please.

ESSENTIAL FISH BURGER

WITH ROCK LING

This fish burger was created as another lockdown comfort meal – born in a time when we were juggling a newborn baby, a toddler and a busy shop. And while we were so thankful to be able to keep working, we didn't have much steam left at the end of those days to get too creative with dinner. This quick meal has remained a fave to this day.

MAKES 2

- 1 × quantity seasoned flour – see Master Recipe for Floured Fried Seafood (page 165)
- 2 rock ling fillets (300–400 g total), skin off (see Notes)
- 4 butter lettuce leaves
- 125 ml (½ cup) olive oil
- 2 soft burger or brioche buns
- Japanese mayonnaise
- 2 gherkin pickles, sliced lengthways
- 4 finely sliced red onion rounds

Place the seasoned flour in a deep bowl. Coat the rock ling fillets and set them aside on some baking paper.

Rinse and pat dry the lettuce leaves and gather the rest of the ingredients together so you are ready to assemble everything when it's time.

Heat the olive oil in a frying pan over medium heat. Fry the rock ling for 2–3 minutes on each side, until the colour is golden and the fish has just cooked through.

Meanwhile, lightly toast the burger buns.

Time to assemble ... spread the mayo on the top and bottom halves of the buns, top with a couple of lettuce leaves, the rock ling, slices of gherkin and red onion. Place the bun lids on top and enjoy.

NOTES Select mid- to tail-end pieces of rock ling that are the same thickness – these will cook more evenly.

You can sub in other fish for this dish like snapper or swordfish.

CRISPY FLATHEAD TACOS

WITH SMOKY CHILLI SLAW

Taco Tuesdays at our place are always seafood! When simply fried fish and really fresh salad come together, it's so, so good. Our go-to is flathead or rock ling, with the obligatory slaw and loads of chilli oil and mayo. This is a great meal to share with friends and make your own as you go.

MAKES 8

1 × quantity seasoned flour – see Master Recipe for Floured Fried Seafood (page 165)
8 small flathead fillets (600 g total), skin off (see Note)
1 carrot, julienned
¼ cabbage, shredded
½ red onion, finely sliced
2 lemons or limes, halved
extra-virgin olive oil for drizzling
1 tablespoon Japanese mayonnaise, plus extra to serve
salt flakes and freshly ground black pepper
smoked chilli oil (optional)
8 soft tacos
125 ml (½ cup) olive oil

Place the seasoned flour in a deep bowl. Coat the flathead fillets in the flour and set aside on some baking paper.

Combine the vegetables in a bowl and dress them with a squeeze of lemon or lime juice, a drizzle of olive oil, the mayonnaise, salt flakes and freshly ground black pepper to taste. If you like a little heat, add some chilli oil here. Combine and set aside.

Wrap the tacos in foil and warm in the oven.

Heat the olive oil in a frying pan over medium heat. Fry the flathead in batches for 3–5 minutes, until the colour is golden and they are cooked through.

We like to lay all the ingredients out on the table – the tacos, salad mix, extra lemons or limes, the flathead and mayo – and put them together ourselves. We always add a drizzle of chilli oil to finish it off.

NOTE You can just as easily use rock ling, prawns or swordfish as an alternative.

PIZZA IN BIANCO

WITH CHILLI & ANCHOVIES

This classic focaccia-style pizza is Nonna Filomena's recipe, which goes way back. No pizza party is complete without at least one of these in rotation at our family gatherings. The salty anchovies, fluffy texture and chilli kick make it an ideal side to a main meal.

SERVES 4 AS A SIDE DISH

PIZZA DOUGH

7 g sachet of instant yeast
½ teaspoon white sugar
450 g pizza 00 flour, plus extra for dusting
1 teaspoon salt flakes
2 tablespoons extra-virgin olive oil

TOPPING

48 g can anchovies in oil
1 teaspoon chilli flakes
extra-virgin olive oil for drizzling

Preheat the oven to 180°C (conventional) and oil a baking tray.

Pour 300 ml of tepid water into a bowl with the yeast and sugar. Leave it to sit for 15 minutes, or until bubbly.

In a large bowl, place the flour and salt. Pour the bubbling yeast mixture and olive oil into the flour and mix until the dough comes together. Knead the dough on your benchtop for around 10 minutes, or until the dough bounces back when you press it. Cover and prove in a warm place until the dough has doubled in size – this will take anywhere from 45 minutes to an hour depending on how warm the room is.

Sprinkle some flour on your benchtop and gently turn the dough out of the bowl. Divide the dough into two portions. Use your fingers to stretch out each piece of dough to a roughly 25 cm round, then place the pieces on the oiled tray.

Top with anchovies, chilli flakes and a good drizzle of olive oil.

Bake in the oven until golden, around 20 minutes.

PASTA & RICE

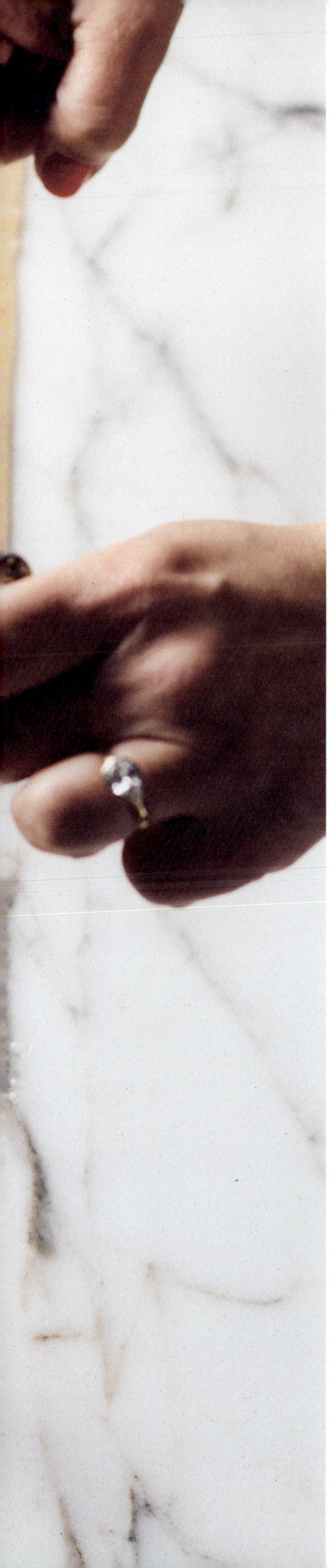

SQUID INK ORECCHIETTE

WITH BUTTERY CRAB SAUCE

Squid ink pasta is rich and delightful. This dish is one that we love to eat during the cooler months – it's hearty and has a certain luxurious quality about it. Orecchiette is lovely to use as it 'catches' the crab like little cups. This version is quick to prepare and best served with a crisp white, in company.

SERVES 2–3

150 g salted butter
200 g cooked crab meat (see Note)
2 tablespoons tomato passata
generous splash of white wine
salt flakes and freshly ground black pepper
300 g fresh squid ink pasta
zest of 1 lemon
chilli oil (optional)

Put a large pot of water on to boil.

In a large frying pan over medium–low heat, gently melt the butter. Stir through the crab meat for 1–2 minutes, letting it warm gently in the butter. Add the tomato passata and cook for another minute. Next, add the wine and allow the alcohol to cook off. Have a taste at this point, season accordingly, then turn off the heat.

When the water is boiling, add a good pinch of salt, let it return to the boil, then pop the squid ink pasta in to cook as per the packet instructions.

Once cooked, quickly strain the pasta, reserving 150 ml of the pasta water in case you need it to loosen the sauce. Add the pasta directly to the pan and stir through. If it seems a little dry, add a splash of the pasta water and keep stirring; this will emulsify with the butter sauce, adding a slight creaminess.

Add the lemon zest here to taste. You want enough to elevate the flavours but not to overpower them.

Plate up into individual bowls and serve immediately. A little chilli oil on top is lovely if you like the heat (optional, of course).

NOTE You could easily swap crab for lobster, bug meat, prawn or vongole.

SPAGHETTI WITH RICOTTA & BOTTARGA

When Laura's dad visits his local cheesemaker, he often brings home freshly made, warm ricotta for everyone in the family. It's completely delicious, the texture is silky, and we just love eating it straight out of the tub. If there is any left over we make this pasta.

SERVES 4

- 400 g spaghetti
- 1 tablespoon extra-virgin olive oil
- 375 g ricotta (ideally freshly made; see Note)
- 1 tablespoon grated pecorino, plus extra to serve
- 2 tablespoons finely grated bottarga

Put a large pot of water on to boil. Once the water is boiling, add a good pinch of salt, let it return to the boil then add the spaghetti.

There is not much more to do at this stage other than set the table!

Once the pasta is cooked al dente, strain and transfer to a large serving dish. Add the olive oil, ricotta and pecorino and combine gently. Top with the grated bottarga and serve. We like to bring the bottarga and the grater to the table to grate a little extra over the individual plates, if desired.

It's that simple!

NOTE If you can find warm, freshly made ricotta, give it a try ... it's heavenly! If you can't, store-bought refrigerated ricotta will work just as well.

RICOTTA & CRAB RAVIOLI WITH TOMATO SUGO

This crab ravioli is a homage to Nonna Filomena's ricotta ravioli – pillowy soft and delightful with a very simple, summery tomato sugo. The sweetness of the crab nestled in the creamy ricotta with a hint of lemon zest is quite sublime. To simplify this recipe you can buy fresh pasta instead of making it.

SERVES 6

FILLING

400 g ricotta (see Notes)
300 g cooked spanner crab meat
zest of 1 lemon
handful of flat-leaf parsley, leaves picked and finely chopped
salt flakes and freshly ground black pepper
2 eggs, beaten

PASTA

400 g 00 flour, plus extra for dusting
4 eggs
1 tablespoon extra-virgin olive oil
salt flakes

TOMATO SUGO

2 tablespoons extra-virgin olive oil
3 garlic cloves, finely chopped
2–3 × 250 g tubs cherry tomatoes
salt flakes and freshly ground black pepper

NOTES Strained ricotta – which is firmer and drier than the one in the container – is best for this. You can find this at a deli or supermarket deli.

Uncooked ravioli can be covered and stored in the fridge for a few hours or frozen to cook at a later date.

If you like a smooth sugo, give it a blitz at the end as pictured (we prefer it chunky).

To make the filling, gently soften the ricotta in a large bowl with a fork. Gently fold through the crab, lemon zest, parsley and some salt and pepper to taste. Add the egg, mix, then set aside in the fridge.

To make the pasta, place the flour in a large bowl. Make a well in the centre, then crack the eggs into the well. Add the oil and a generous pinch of salt. Using a fork, beat the eggs until smooth. Mix the flour little by little into the egg well until it binds – it shouldn't be sticky. Flour the work surface and your hands, then turn the dough out of the bowl. Knead the dough until it's smooth, silky and elastic. Cover it with a tea towel and leave to rest for 30 minutes.

Dust a large plate or baking tray with some flour. Divide the dough into four pieces and stretch them out with your hands so they are wide enough to fit into a pasta machine. Feed the pieces in one at a time (keep the others covered with a clean tea towel). Roll through the machine, fold and repeat until the sheet is around 60–70 cm long and around 2–3 mm thick. You may need to do this three or four times. Lay the pasta sheet on the dusted plate. Keep going until all the sheets are ready.

Dust another large plate or baking tray with some flour. Place a teaspoon of filling onto a pasta sheet, leaving a 2–3 cm margin at the side and bottom of the sheet. Work in a horizontal line across the short edge, spooning filling at intervals of around 5–6 cm and repeat for the length of the sheet. Fold the pasta lengthways to cover the filling. Working from the middle outwards using your fingers, press and gently seal the pasta around the filling, making sure to work out any air pockets. Using a pasta cutter, create a half-moon shape about 5 cm wide, then use a fork to press and seal. Place the ravioli on the prepared plate or tray as you go. Repeat with the remaining three pasta sheets.

To make the sugo, place the olive oil and garlic in a large, cold saucepan and turn the heat to medium. Once you can smell the garlic, add the tomatoes and reduce the heat to low. Allow the tomatoes to cook down gently for around 10–15 minutes. Add salt and pepper to taste. Set aside.

Put a large pot of water on to boil. Once the water is boiling, add a good pinch of salt, let it return to the boil, then gently place the ravioli in using a slotted spoon. Cook the ravioli until they rise to the surface of the water, around 3–5 minutes, then remove them one by one with the slotted spoon. Divide the ravioli among plates, spoon the tomato sugo on top and serve.

LINGUINE MARINARA

A classic favourite on the Italian side of the family! Anthony cuts marinara fresh every day for the store, sometimes two or three times. It's a simple mix of fresh seafood, including salmon, rock ling, prawns and vongole. Depending on what seafood is in season, he might add tuna or swordfish too.

We like our marinara in 'bianco', but some prefer it with a little tomato.

SERVES 2

- 2 tablespoons extra-virgin olive oil
- 3–4 garlic cloves, finely chopped
- 2–3 anchovies
- 1 small red chilli, deseeded and finely chopped (optional)
- 200 g cherry tomatoes (optional)
- 250 g linguine or spaghetti
- 400–500 g marinara mix (ours includes salmon, rock ling, vongole and prawns)
- 125 ml (½ cup) white wine
- 1 teaspoon salted butter
- salt flakes and freshly ground black pepper
- zest of 1 lemon (optional)
- ½ bunch of flat-leaf parsley, leaves picked and chopped (optional)

Put a large pot of water on to boil.

In a large pan (or a wok), heat the olive oil on medium heat. Add the garlic, anchovies and some chilli, if you like, and cook down until the garlic is gently browned and the anchovies have disintegrated. (If you like a little tomato, add the cherry tomatoes here and allow them to cook down.)

Once the water is boiling add a good pinch of salt, let it return to the boil, then add the pasta.

Add the seafood to the pan with the garlic mixture, stirring occasionally to ensure it cooks evenly. After about 10 minutes, the seafood will be almost cooked and will release a bit of water. Remove the seafood gently with a slotted spoon and set aside. Simmer the liquid for 5–10 minutes to allow it to reduce. Add the wine and cook off the alcohol so that you are left with a thin sauce. Add the seafood back to the pan at this point to cook for another 3–5 minutes, or until plump and cooked through but still intact. Now is the time to add the butter and season to taste.

Strain the pasta, reserving 125 ml (½ cup) of the pasta water in case you need it to loosen the sauce. Add the pasta directly to the large pan with the seafood and stir through. If it seems a bit dry, splash a little of the reserved pasta water in while you are stirring. Top with the lemon zest and parsley, if using, and mix through.

Transfer to a large bowl or individual bowls and it's ready to serve.

CREAMY CRAYFISH PASTA

This rich and deeply satisfying crayfish pasta dish was born from the leftover cray in those lockdown days, when we would pump out over a hundred prawn and cray rolls in the store and there was always some to spare!

SERVES 4

1 tablespoon extra-virgin olive oil
3 garlic cloves, finely chopped
100 g salted butter (lots of butter!)
125 ml (½ cup) white wine
150 ml pure cream or crème fraîche
250 g cooked cray meat (see Note)
salt flakes and freshly ground black pepper
zest of 1 lemon
400 g spaghetti

Put a large pot of water on to boil.

In a cold saucepan, pour in the oil and add the garlic, turn the heat on low and cook gently for 1–2 minutes. Add the butter. Once the butter is melted, add the wine and allow the alcohol to cook off.

Pour in the cream and add the cray to warm through. Season to taste with salt and pepper and add the lemon zest. Take off the heat and set aside.

Once the water is boiling, add a good pinch of salt, let it return to the boil, then pop the pasta in.

Once the pasta is cooked al dente, strain the pasta, reserving 250 ml (1 cup) of the pasta water in case you need it to loosen the sauce. Add the pasta to the creamy sauce in the pan. Mix through, adding a little more moisture from the pasta water as you need it. Keep stirring until all the pasta is coated and creamy.

Transfer the pasta to a large platter and serve.

NOTE You can use raw cray for this recipe – you'll just need to cook it a little longer, about 6–8 minutes, until bright white and firm. Moreton Bay bugs or crab will work for this dish too.

PASTA WITH SCALLOPS

AGLIO E OLIO

This simple pasta is a riff on a classic pasta aglio e olio and was Laura's childhood favourite. If you're Melbourne-based, local scallops from Bass Strait are in season from late July to December and are so perfect for this. Traditionally, we always make this with spaghetti, but feel free to experiment with different pastas as we have here with mafaldine.

SERVES 4

- 3 tablespoons extra-virgin olive oil, plus a little extra for drizzling
- 3 garlic cloves, finely chopped
- 250 g local scallops, roe on and cleaned (see Note)
- 400 g mafaldine
- 30 g salted butter
- zest and juice of 1 lemon
- 1 small bunch of flat-leaf parsley, leaves picked and finely chopped
- salt flakes and freshly ground black pepper

Put a large pot of water on to boil.

In a cold saucepan, pour in the oil and add the garlic, turn the heat on low and cook gently for 2–3 minutes. Once you can smell that garlic aroma, turn the heat up a little to medium, drop in the scallops and cook for around 3–4 minutes. They will firm up and shrink as they cook. If they let out a lot of water, we suggest removing them from the pan with a slotted spoon, placing them aside and reducing the liquid by half before returning them to the pan.

Once the water is boiling, add a good pinch of salt, let it return to the boil, then pop the pasta in to cook.

Add the butter, lemon zest and most of the parsley to the pan with the scallops and stir through. Add salt flakes and freshly ground black pepper to taste. If it needs a little more moisture, add a small drizzle of oil. Set aside off the heat while the pasta finishes cooking.

Strain the pasta, reserving 150 ml of the pasta water in case you need it to loosen the sauce. Pour the pasta into the scallop sauce and gently mix through. Add the lemon juice to taste, the remaining parsley and a little more oil if required, so that the pasta is well coated. You can add in some of the pasta water here if the sauce seems a little dry, and stir through to emulsify. Serve immediately and enjoy.

NOTE You can use frozen scallops, but they will release a lot of water in the cooking process. If you can't easily access scallops, prawns will also work well.

CHRISTMAS EVE

CHERRY TOMATO & CRAB PASTA

This dish represents the beginning of the festive season for us. It's our Christmas Eve starter, but it's just as special for a dinner at home with friends. It's so easy to prepare and we love how the cherry tomatoes caramelise – cooked gently and slowly, these are so flavourful.

SERVES 4 AS A STARTER

500 g cherry tomatoes
4 garlic cloves, skin on
200 ml extra-virgin olive oil
salt flakes and freshly ground black pepper
400–500 g linguine (or spaghetti)
200 g cooked spanner crab (or any crab meat, crayfish or bug meat)
zest and juice of ½ lemon

Preheat the oven to 150°C (conventional).

Arrange the cherry tomatoes and garlic cloves in a baking dish, splash generously with the olive oil and season with salt and pepper to taste – this will be the base of your sauce. Bake in the oven for around 30–40 minutes, until the cherry tomatoes darken and soften.

Just before the tomatoes are ready, put a pot of water on to boil. Once the water is boiling, add a good pinch of salt, let it return to the boil, then add the linguine.

While the pasta is cooking, take the tomatoes out of the oven and remove the garlic. Add the crab, then the lemon zest and stir through gently. This will warm the crab. Check the oil here – does it seem like enough to coat your pasta? If not, be sure to keep aside 150 ml of the pasta water before you drain your linguine (to stir through and add a little something extra to your sauce).

Once cooked al dente, drain the pasta and transfer to a large bowl. Pour the crab and cherry tomato sauce on top (add a little of the pasta water here if needed) and stir through to coat the pasta. Add a squeeze of lemon juice here if you like a bit more zing, or more zest.

Serve immediately, with a cheers to the season.

PASTA VONGOLE

AGLIO E OLIO

A pasta classic that will transport you to the Italian coast and endless summer days. This quick and simple to prepare dish has few ingredients, which really lets the vongole shine. Best enjoyed in company!

SERVES 2

2 tablespoons olive oil, plus extra for serving
3 garlic cloves, finely chopped
zest of 1 lemon
2 teaspoons salted butter
500 g vongole (or pipis)
150 ml white wine
250 g linguine
salt flakes and freshly ground black pepper
chilli oil (optional)

Put a large pot of water on to boil.

In a large saucepan on medium heat, add the olive oil, garlic, lemon zest and butter and gently sauté until aromatic. Drop in the vongole and white wine, cover with a lid and leave to cook until the vongole open – around 3–5 minutes. Allow them all to open, then remove from the heat, taking the lid off.

Once the pasta water is boiling, add a good pinch of salt, let it return to the boil, then pop the pasta in to cook.

Once the pasta is cooked al dente, strain it, reserving 125 ml (½ cup) of the pasta water. Place the pasta in a serving bowl and pour the vongole on top. Use tongs to stir the pasta and slowly add the pasta water, stirring continuously to create a nice emulsion.

Season to taste with salt flakes and freshly ground black pepper, and ensure you have a side bowl to collect the shells. Allow everyone to help themselves – we always have extra olive oil and chilli oil to serve on the table.

THE BEST SEAFOOD FOR FISH STOCK

Choose a lighter fish for more subtle flavours. For a stronger, more robust stock, use lobster and prawn heads. Ask your fishmonger what they have available, fresh or frozen.

HĀPUKU COLLAR

LOBSTER

MONKFISH

PRAWN HEADS

TUNA RISOTTO

WITH TOMATO & OLIVES

Laura's mum would throw this together as a one-pot midweek dinner in the winter months. It's filling and warming, perfect for feeding a family, and one of those comfort meals you will come back to time and again.

SERVES 3–4

- 2 litres fish or vegetable stock (cubes or store-bought are fine for this recipe)
- 2 tablespoons extra-virgin olive oil
- 1 small brown onion, finely chopped
- 2–3 anchovies
- 1 small red chilli, deseeded and finely chopped (optional)
- 250 g arborio rice
- 125 ml (½ cup) white wine
- 400 g can chopped tomatoes
- 425 g can tuna in olive oil, drained
- handful of pitted kalamata olives
- 1 teaspoon salted butter
- 50 g grated pecorino, plus extra to serve
- ½ bunch of flat-leaf parsley, leaves picked and chopped
- zest of 1 lemon
- salt flakes and freshly ground black pepper

Prepare the stock in a pot on the stove and keep it simmering gently on the lowest heat.

Heat the olive oil in a large non-stick saucepan over medium heat. Add the onion, anchovies and some chilli if you like, and cook down until the onion has softened and the anchovies have disintegrated.

Add the arborio rice and gently brown for 2–3 minutes, stirring, then add the wine, allowing the alcohol to cook off. Add the tomato next. Once the moisture has all been absorbed by the rice, start to add the stock, one ladle at a time, allowing it to absorb before adding more. Keep repeating this for around 15–20 minutes until the rice is al dente and almost done. Remember to keep stirring so the rice doesn't stick.

Add the tuna and olives to the pot, stirring through. At this point we like to add a last ladle of stock, turn off the heat and pop a lid on (slightly ajar) to finish off the cooking process. You want the risotto to have a slight firmness and not be mushy.

After letting the risotto sit in the pot for 5 minutes, add the butter, pecorino, parsley, lemon zest and seasoning, to taste, then stir through.

Place the pot directly on the table and serve into individual bowls ... a second plate is obligatory, as is an extra sprinkle of pecorino.

EASY ONE-POT

SEAFOOD RICE

This recipe comes from Laura's sister, Liza (our much loved 'zia'), who is a wonderful cook. A simple take on a paella, this is an easy but impressive dish, ideal for entertaining. A mix of seafood and the heady green of the parsley is something you can tweak according to your palate; the greener the better we say!

SERVES 4

3 tablespoons extra-virgin olive oil, plus extra for drizzling
1 small brown onion (or 2 shallots), finely chopped
10 garlic cloves, peeled and finely chopped
1 litre fish stock
1 bunch of flat-leaf parsley, leaves picked and chopped
salt flakes
400 g Calasparra, bomba or arborio rice
1 rock ling fillet (250–300 g), skin off, cut into bite-sized pieces
300 g fresh calamari hoods, including tentacles, cleaned and chopped
300 g raw prawn cutlets, tails on
300 g mussels, cleaned and debearded (see Note)
freshly ground black pepper

Heat the olive oil on medium–low heat in a large non-stick pan with a lid. Sauté the onion for 1–2 minutes, then add the garlic and cook for 1 minute more. Add the stock, most of the parsley and salt to taste, then bring to a gentle boil.

Sprinkle the rice into the stock and simmer for 6–7 minutes, stirring.

Add the rock ling and calamari, shaking the pan so they sink down into the rice and stock. Now add the prawns and mussels, cover with the lid, and allow to cook for around 12 minutes on medium–low.

Take the lid off and taste the rice to ensure it is cooked through. You will know the dish is ready when the rice is softened with a slight firmness, the mussels have opened and the prawns have curled and turned pink. If not, let it cook a little longer. Season with salt and pepper to taste, drizzle with some olive oil and sprinkle generously with the remaining parsley. Stir to combine.

Place the cooking vessel in the middle of the table and serve individual plates directly from the pan. Make sure each serve gets a share of crunchy rice from the bottom and a good variety of the seafood.

NOTE You can sub in vongole, clams or pipis for the mussels.

GREEK-INSPIRED PILAF

WITH OCEAN TROUT & CRÈME FRAÎCHE

During the cooler months, we often make spanakorizo – a traditional vegetarian Greek dish made with spinach and rice. This pilaf has its heart in that dish. We like to flake the ocean trout through the rice and serve with a little extra crème fraîche and dill fronds on top. It's heavenly.

SERVES 4

- 2 tablespoons extra-virgin olive oil, plus extra for brushing
- 1 small brown onion, finely chopped
- 200 g medium-grain rice
- handful of dill fronds, chopped, plus extra to serve
- 200 g frozen peas
- salt flakes and freshly ground black pepper
- 2 ocean trout fillets (400 g total), skin on (see Notes)
- 3 tablespoons crème fraîche, plus extra to serve
- zest and juice of 1 lemon

You will need a pan with a lid or a Dutch oven.

Place the olive oil and brown onion in the cold pan and turn the heat on to medium. Once the oil is warmed, cook the onion until it has softened. Add the rice and cook, just long enough to add a little colour.

Add the dill, then cover with around 1 litre of water (it should sit 1–2 cm above the rice). Add the peas and a little salt and pepper to taste, then stir and place the lid on.

It should take around 15 minutes to cook the rice gently via absorption – check it every few minutes, give it a gentle stir and add a little more water if needed.

While the rice is cooking, prepare the trout by brushing it with a little olive oil and seasoning with some salt.

Heat a non-stick frying pan over medium heat. Place the trout skin-side down in the pan and fry for 2–3 minutes, until crisp, then turn over and cook for another 2–3 minutes. Remove the trout from the pan and rest for a few minutes. Once rested, remove the skin and discard. Flake the trout by hand, then set aside.

By this stage the rice should be just about done. Taste the rice to check it is cooked through. Stir through the crème fraîche and lemon zest. Taste and adjust the seasoning here and, if needed, add some of the lemon juice. Remove from the heat and stir the flaked trout through.

To serve, spoon the rice into four bowls and top with a dollop of crème fraîche and some dill fronds.

NOTES If you prefer, you can bake the trout in the oven or an air fryer on 180°C (conventional) until cooked through.

You can substitute the trout for salmon, or even hot smoked trout or hot smoked salmon instead of fresh fish if you like.

ON THE BARBECUE

THE BEST SEAFOOD FOR THE BARBECUE

Choose something that won't 'stick' to the barbecue. If you have a flat plate the options can be endless!

CALAMARI

HĀPUKU COLLAR

LOBSTER

MORETON BAY BUGS

OCTOPUS
PRAWNS
SWORDFISH
BLUE-EYE
SNAPPER

BARBECUED CALAMARI

WITH LEMON & OLIVE OIL DRESSING

This recipe really showcases good produce – and calamari is the star of this show. The cooking and prep time for this recipe is minimal, making it a summertime favourite. We make this regularly as an appetiser, but it can easily be scaled up with a salad to make a main meal, or served as part of a big seafood barbecue.

SERVES 2

- 2 calamari hoods (400 g), including tentacles, cleaned (see Note)
- 1–2 tablespoons extra-virgin olive oil, plus extra for drizzling
- salt flakes
- 1 lemon, halved
- 2 tablespoons chopped flat-leaf parsley leaves

To prepare the calamari, pull the tentacles out of the hood, where they join – they will slide out with a little resistance. Cut off the bulbous head and discard. The tentacles should all come loose. Rinse them and set aside on paper towel to dry. Place your hand inside the hood and remove any loose skin or innards, then rinse and pat dry with paper towel. Butterfly the squid hoods by cutting down one side of the hood to open it up, creating one flat piece. Next, score the hoods in a pineapple or criss-cross sequence. This ensures the hoods don't curl when cooking.

Brush the hoods with some extra-virgin olive oil, season with some salt flakes and place on a hot grill. A charcoal barbecue is preferred but a normal one is fine also.

The calamari will char and cook quickly – keep an eye on it so it does not burn. Cook for 2–3 minutes on each side. The cooked calamari should be a bright white, speckled with charring.

Take the calamari off the grill, slice it into bite-sized pieces, then plate it up with a good squeeze of lemon, a drizzle of olive oil, a sprinkle of parsley and some salt flakes.

NOTE Fresh calamari works best here. You can ask your fishmonger to clean it for you. If you do buy it cleaned, ensure the flesh is a bright white with no redness (or fire, as we call it in the trade), which indicates it's past its prime.

BARBECUED PRAWNS

COOKED WHOLE

There is nothing more Australian than a prawn on the barbie! It's one of a few ways we eat prawns in our house during the warmer months. A good size for cooking on the barbecue is a U10 or a U8 grading. Always choose Aussie prawns. Cheaper prawns tend to be imported and have little flavour.

SERVES 4

12 raw king prawns (see Notes)
2 tablespoons extra-virgin olive oil
1–2 lemons, cut in half, plus extra to serve
handful of flat-leaf parsley leaves, chopped, to serve (optional)

Warm your barbecue or a griddle pan to medium heat.

Rinse the prawns, then pat them dry with some paper towel. Massage some olive oil into the prawns, making sure they are well coated.

Place the prawns onto the heat. When they change to a pinkish colour it's time to turn them over – just a few minutes on each side will do. Don't overcook them or the shell will stick to the prawn meat, making them hard to peel (but no less delicious!).

When they are ready, place them on a serving plate and douse them with a good squeeze of lemon juice (hang onto those lemons to rinse the smell off your hands!). Add a little parsley if you fancy.

We prefer to peel our prawns after they are cooked. It's a bit messy but, really, it's the most delicious way, and every table usually has a designated prawn peeler, don't they? Have some extra lemon for squeezing and a bowl of water with chopped lemon for rinsing your hands at the table.

NOTES A U10 prawn is a good average size (we never stock anything smaller) and you will get approximately 22 prawns per kilo. A U8 prawn is a larger size with approximately 18 per kilo.

You can just as easily swap the prawns for bugs or another crustacean.

BARBECUED PRAWNS
COOKED WHOLE

BARBECUED CALAMARI WITH LEMON & OLIVE OIL DRESSING

OCTOPUS ON THE BARBECUE

WITH LEMON & OLIVE OIL

This is a classic dish that we enjoy around the barbecue over the summer months. It's a really simple way to prepare octopus. The chewiness of the octopus is offset with the charred texture and the tangy lemon juice. This heavenly dish disappears fast!

SERVES 4 AS AN APPETISER

- 500 g tenderised octopus tentacles (fresh or frozen)
- extra-virgin olive oil for basting and serving
- salt flakes and freshly ground black pepper
- 2 lemons, cut in half
- handful of flat-leaf parsley leaves, chopped

Place the tentacles on a large plate, drizzle with olive oil and season well with salt flakes and freshly ground black pepper. Massage the octopus to ensure it's well coated, then leave it to sit for 20 minutes before placing on the grill.

The octopus is best cooked on a charcoal barbecue, when the embers settle so there is no live flame. Cook for 15–20 minutes, turning once or twice, until it is nicely charred and has taken on the smokiness of the charcoal.

Transfer the octopus from the grill to a chopping board and cut into bite-sized pieces.

Place the octopus pieces on a serving dish, then squeeze over the juice of one lemon, add a drizzle of olive oil and sprinkle with the fresh parsley. Add a little more salt if needed.

Serve with the extra lemon on the side.

BARBECUED SALMON

WITH SMOKY CHILLI SLAW

Salmon is the most popular of all seafood species these days, with its health benefits and rich flavour. Good-quality salmon needs little to shine; here we simply grill it on the barbecue. The smoky chilli dressing combined with crunchy slaw and the barbecued salmon makes this easy-to-prepare dish a hit in summer.

SERVES 2

- 2 salmon fillets (400 g total), skin on (see Notes)
- salt flakes
- 300 g white and red cabbage, finely sliced
- 1 carrot, grated
- ½ red onion, finely sliced
- ½ cup Japanese mayonnaise
- juice of 1 lime (or lemon), plus extra to serve
- 1 tablespoon extra-virgin olive oil
- smoky jalapeño chilli sauce (we like the Tuckshop brand), to taste
- sea salt and freshly ground black pepper

Prepare your barbecue – the flat plate is best for grilling fillets. Salt the salmon and set aside.

Place the cabbage, carrot and onion in a large bowl. In another bowl, prepare the dressing by combining the mayonnaise, lime juice, extra-virgin olive oil, smoky chilli sauce and salt and pepper to taste. Taste as you go to get the heat and tanginess just right. When you're happy with the dressing, pour it over the slaw and combine. Set aside.

Place the salmon onto the grill skin-side down and cook for 3–4 minutes. Turn and finish off for another 1–2 minutes. The skin should be browned and crispy with a little pink in the centre of the flesh. Leave to rest for 1–2 minutes.

Divide the slaw between two plates, top with the crispy-skinned salmon and another squeeze of lime if you like, then serve.

NOTES This will work just as well on a frying pan but it will not have the smokiness of the barbecue.

White fish like hāpuku or blue-eye will also work well for this dish.

SIMPLE BAKES

BLUE-EYE PARCEL

WITH XO SAUCE

This may be one of our all-time favourite seafood meals! Anthony is a big fan of Asian food and one-pan dishes, so this ticks all the boxes for a simple and flavourful meal ready to eat in under an hour. The XO sauce is the key ingredient – the better quality you can find, the more rewarding this will be. And of course it's a lovely dish to share table-side.

SERVES 2–3

1 blue-eye fillet (500–600 g), skin on

100 g XO sauce

1 tablespoon sesame oil

1 tablespoon soy sauce

freshly ground black pepper

1 carrot, julienned

2 spring onions, finely chopped, plus extra to serve

steamed jasmine rice, to serve

Preheat the oven to 180°C (conventional).

Lay the blue-eye on a large piece of baking paper on a baking tray (you need to be generous with the baking paper as you want to be able to create a pocket for the fish to steam in; you want the paper to be roughly twice the length of the fish).

Pour the XO over the fish and rub it into the flesh so it's all coated. Drizzle on the sesame oil and soy sauce, then add a little black pepper. (We don't salt the fish as the sauce is quite salty.) Add the carrot and spring onion.

Close up the parcel like an envelope to create a little steam chamber.

Place in the oven and bake for around 30 minutes. Once cooked, the blue-eye will be a bright white and the veggies will have softened.

Serve the blue-eye at the table, opening the aromatic parcel and serving directly into individual bowls with some rice on the side. Top with a little extra spring onion.

SESAME PRAWN SAUSAGE ROLLS

This riff on the classic prawn toast was born of Anthony's love of Asian cuisine and the search for a new winter option to add to our in-store offerings. It's a recipe we're excited to share, and a great one to make and freeze for a quick snack or entertaining.

MAKES 8

500 g raw prawn meat, finely chopped or minced
60 g breadcrumbs
2–3 spring onions, finely chopped
1 shallot, grated (or ½ small onion)
3 garlic cloves, grated
1 teaspoon grated ginger
1 egg white
50 ml sesame oil
2 teaspoons hoisin
1 tablespoon cornflour
1–2 teaspoons soy sauce
155 g sesame seeds
2 sheets puff pastry
1 egg, beaten, for egg wash
sweet chilli sauce or sriracha, to serve

Preheat the oven to 200°C (conventional) and line a baking tray with baking paper.

Place the prawn meat in a large bowl with the breadcrumbs, spring onion, shallot, garlic, ginger, egg white, sesame oil, hoisin, cornflour and soy sauce. Mix to combine.

Place the sesame seeds in a shallow bowl.

Cut each puff pastry sheet into quarters and divide the prawn mix equally among the pastry pieces, rolling the mixture into a sausage shape in the centre of each piece. Brush the edges with egg wash, then roll the pastry up to create the rolls. Brush the rolls with egg wash and dip the top side into the sesame seeds.

Transfer to the baking tray and bake for around 20 minutes, until golden.

Remove from the oven and leave to cool a little before serving with some sweet chilli sauce or sriracha.

NOTE You can adjust the quantities to suit your palate and scale up for a crowd.

CRUNCHY FISH KIEV

WITH HERB BUTTER

This is one of those nostalgic dishes that takes us back to our 80s childhoods, when chicken Kiev was all the rage. This version became a lockdown winter fave for us, on high rotation in our home and in the store. Served with a simple side of peas or beans and a nice glass of wine, this is the ultimate comfort food.

SERVES 2

- 2 chunky, even-width portions firm white fish (400–500 g total), skin off (we use rock ling)
- 300 g plain flour mixed with 1 teaspoon sea salt and 1 teaspoon freshly ground black pepper
- 3 eggs, beaten
- 200 g panko or other good-quality breadcrumbs
- 125 ml (½ cup) olive oil
- steamed peas or beans, to serve

HERB BUTTER

- 100 g salted butter, softened
- 2 garlic cloves, grated
- ¼ bunch of flat-leaf parsley, leaves picked and finely chopped
- 1 tablespoon finely grated lemon zest

Preheat the oven to 180°C (conventional). Line a baking tray with baking paper.

First up, prepare your herb butter. Place the butter, garlic, parsley and lemon zest in a small mixing bowl and fold together until combined. Lay a piece of plastic wrap on your benchtop, then heap the butter on top. Wrap and roll the butter into a log shape and pop aside in the fridge.

Next, prepare the fish. Pat it dry with paper towel to remove any excess moisture. With a sharp knife, make a 3 cm deep incision on the side of one fillet. Fill with half of the herb butter. Repeat with the second fillet.

Place the seasoned flour, eggs and breadcrumbs into three separate deep dishes, side by side.

Flour each piece of fish, shaking off the excess. Place into the egg, coating well and allowing the excess to drip off, then into the crumb. Pat the crumb so it sticks well to the egg. To create a crunchy outer crust on your Kiev we suggest creating a double crumb. Pop the fish back into the egg, shake off any excess, and then back into the crumb for a second time.

Shallow fry in olive oil on medium heat for 2–3 minutes each side until light golden, then pop the fish onto the baking tray and place in the oven for around 10 minutes to finish. The fish will be a medium golden colour and have a crunchy crust.

Serve on individual plates with simply cooked peas or beans on the side.

MISO-MARINATED SALMON

& VEGGIE RICE BOWLS

This super-nourishing bowl is perfect for lunch or dinner. Our sushi chef, Shirow, prepares salmon in the Japanese method for us to sell in the store. Traditionally, the salmon is marinated in miso for 5–7 days, but if you don't have that much time, 2–3 days will work too.

We serve this rice bowl with whatever vegetables we have on hand and that's the beauty of it – you can create this from what you have with rice and salmon as the base.

SERVES 2

- 2 salmon fillets (300–400 g total), skin on (see Notes)
- salt flakes
- 250 g white miso
- 1½ tablespoons cooking rice wine or sake
- 2 teaspoons soy sauce
- 1½ tablespoons mirin
- 2 teaspoons brown sugar (or honey)
- steamed white rice, to serve
- 50 g edamame, shelled and steamed or thawed
- 1 bunch of broccolini, steamed
- togarashi seasoning or sesame seeds, to serve
- soy sauce, to serve

Start by lightly salting the fish, then set it aside in the fridge for 30 minutes. This will draw out any moisture.

In a medium bowl, combine the miso, cooking rice wine, soy sauce, mirin and sugar.

Once the fish is ready, pat it dry with paper towel to remove any excess moisture.

Pour the marinade into a large shallow dish or plastic container. Add the fish to the container and turn it over to coat each piece evenly. Cover the dish with plastic wrap and place in the fridge to marinate for 24–48 hours.

Halfway through the marinating time, remove the fish and set aside, re-mix the marinade in the dish, then place the salmon back in (turned over), ensuring it is all well coated.

When you are ready to cook the salmon, preheat the oven to 180°C (conventional) and line a baking tray with baking paper.

Place the salmon on the prepared tray, skin-side up, and bake for around 18 minutes, or until the salmon is browned and sticky. Allow it to cool before flaking.

In the meantime, prepare two bowls with steamed rice and place the vegetables on top. Add the salmon, some togarashi or sesame seeds and soy, then serve.

NOTES Ensure you buy very fresh, good-quality salmon for this recipe – fresh salmon should not have any odour.

You can freeze the marinated salmon for up to 1 month.

BLUE-EYE PARCELS

WITH A HERB & DUKKAH CRUST

This was one of those dishes born from foraging in the pantry. The dukkah mixed with the freshness of parsley, garlic and lemon makes for an outstanding and fragrant seasoning for seafood. We love baking this one on the Weber, but it works just as well in the oven. We adore this dish and hope you do also.

SERVES 2–3

- 60 g (⅓ cup) good-quality dukkah
- ⅓ bunch of flat-leaf parsley, leaves picked and chopped
- zest and juice of ½ lemon
- pinch of freshly ground black pepper
- 2 blue-eye fillets (500–600 g total), skin on (see Note)
- 100 ml extra-virgin olive oil

Preheat the oven to 180°C (conventional) or prepare your Weber.

In a bowl, place the dukkah, parsley, lemon zest (reserve the juice for serving) and black pepper, mix gently to combine and set aside.

With a paper towel, pat dry the blue-eye fillets to remove any moisture. Lay two generous lengths of baking paper on a baking tray. You'll need enough baking paper to create parcels that will hold the fish while cooking.

Spoon some of the olive oil over one of the fillets, coating it lightly. Use your fingers to rub the oil in. This creates a base for the dukkah mix. Sprinkle half of the mix over the fish and add another drizzle of olive oil. Fold the paper over the fish and twist the ends like a bon bon. Repeat with the other fillet.

Cook in the oven or Weber for around 20 minutes, or until the fish has cooked through to a bright white. It should be aromatic and moist. Leave it to sit in the parcel until ready to serve – just open it up slightly to release the steam to stop it from continuing to cook.

Open the aromatic parcels at the table and serve directly onto individual plates, making sure everyone gets plenty of the dukkah crust. Add a good squeeze of lemon and serve with some boiled potatoes or a light salad as a side. This is a nice dish for a Sunday lunch.

NOTE Snapper or red emperor would also work well for this recipe.

OCEAN TROUT ALMONDINE

The idea for this dish came from a customer recounting his love of eating trout this way – we just had to try it! The delicate texture of the trout in contrast to the richness of the butter and the nuttiness of the almonds is quite something. This quick and easy dish is lovely with a side of green beans and some mashed potato or a simple salad.

SERVES 2

- 2 ocean trout fillets (400 g total), skin on
- 1 tablespoon extra-virgin olive oil
- salt flakes and freshly ground black pepper
- 2–3 tablespoons salted butter
- 120 g slivered or flaked almonds
- juice of 1 lemon
- handful of flat-leaf parsley leaves, chopped

Preheat a large non-stick frying pan over medium heat.

While the pan warms, pat the trout dry with paper towel, brush with a little olive oil and season with a little salt and pepper.

Place the trout skin-side down in the hot pan and fry for 3–5 minutes, until the skin is crisp and the colour is soft pink. Turn the fillets over and finish off for around 2 minutes. (You can place a fish weight on top to ensure an even cook – see Note.)

Remove the fillets from the pan and set aside to rest on two serving plates.

In a small pan over medium–low heat, add the butter and allow it to melt. Continue to cook the butter, while stirring, until it has browned, then add the almonds. Remove from the heat and add the lemon juice.

Pour the hot brown butter and almonds over the trout, top with parsley and serve immediately with your choice of sides.

NOTE A fish weight (or meat weight) is really helpful to ensure even cooking, especially for uneven portions like trout and salmon. The weight helps to disperse the heat through the thicker part of the portion, encouraging more even cooking.

BARRAMUNDI CURRY PARCELS

We went through a big phase of cooking en papillote (baking in paper). It's such an easy and satisfying way to prepare fish – it only takes 30–40 minutes from start to finish. This recipe is a little hotpot of goodness that's really easy to cook for one or two. The flavour options are endless with en papillote, but here we've opted for a beautiful curried barramundi with fried shallots.

SERVES 2

1 tablespoon vegetable oil
100–120 g good-quality curry paste (we prefer a red or green Thai curry with a nice amount of heat)
250 ml can coconut milk
2 portions barramundi fillet (400 g total), skin off (see Note)
125 g green beans, chopped (optional)
250 g bamboo shoots
steamed basmati rice, to serve
½ cup fried shallots, to serve

Preheat the oven to 180°C (conventional).

In a wok, heat the oil over medium heat and fry off the curry paste until aromatic. Add the coconut milk and bring it to a gentle simmer, then take off the heat.

Lay two generous lengths of baking paper on a baking tray. You'll need enough baking paper to create a parcel that will hold the fish while cooking.

Add a little of the curry mix to the bottom of each baking paper vessel and place the barramundi fillets on top. If you want to add some green beans here, layer them on top of the fish with the bamboo shoots.

Add more curry on top of the fish and seal the papillote like an envelope, scrunching it together along the seam to create a little steam chamber. Repeat with the second fillet (if there is any extra curry, serve it at the table with the fish).

Bake in the oven for 20 minutes. When ready, the barramundi will be fluffy and a bright white colour, and the curry will be aromatic.

Once cooked, remove the parcels from the oven and let them sit for 1–2 minutes before creating an opening for the steam to escape.

Divide the steamed rice between two plates and portion the fish and vegetables between them. Top with the fried shallots.

NOTE You can just as easily use rock ling, monkfish, blue-eye or snapper here, or add another vegetable of your choice rather than green beans.

BAKED SNAPPER FILLETS

ON A BED OF LEMONY POTATOES

This one-tray meal is delicious – the combination of potatoes and delicate snapper fillets with a lemony tang is just sublime. Ensure you slice your potatoes thinly to promote a quick cooking time and maximum crunch. You can easily sub in other white fish for this one, like ling or whiting.

SERVES 4

extra-virgin olive oil

3 large unpeeled potatoes, finely sliced (see Notes)

1 lemon, finely sliced

1 red onion, finely sliced in rounds

salt flakes and freshly ground black pepper

4 snapper fillets (500–600 g total), skin on

1 tablespoon chopped thyme or flat-leaf parsley leaves, to serve

2 lemons, cut in half, for squeezing and serving (optional)

Preheat the oven to 180°C (conventional) and grease the base of a large baking dish with extra-virgin olive oil.

Layer slices of potato, lemon (reserve a few slices of lemon for topping) and onion around the dish, overlapping as you go. Season with a little salt and pepper and brush the potatoes with olive oil.

Place the potatoes in the oven to bake for around 30–40 minutes until golden and crunchy.

Pat the snapper fillets dry with paper towel and lightly season with a pinch of salt.

Retrieve the baking dish from the oven and place the fillets evenly on top of the potatoes, adding a few lemon slices on top of the fish. Return to the oven and cook for another 5 minutes. The snapper should be white and fluffy once cooked through.

Remove the dish from the oven, sprinkle with the thyme or parsley and add a squeeze of lemon. Serve straight from the baking dish to individual plates, with the lemon halves on the side if you like it more lemony. A simple green salad is a nice accompaniment.

NOTES Using a mandoline is an easy way to ensure your potato slices are even.

If you like, you can add a few cherry tomatoes to this bake to bring another element of flavour.

BAKED RAINBOW TROUT WITH BREAD & OLIVES

Baked whole fish is mostly how we ate fish growing up, much to our dismay at the time. We are so thankful to our parents for pushing us to eat things with scales and bones as kids, as we now have a great appreciation for all types of seafood. Mum would buy a few rainbow trout from the local Greek fishmonger and pull together an oven meal after a long day at work. Rainbow trout is an affordable, readily available freshwater fish that ticks over in our store – and it's delicious. Baked trout is lovely with a side of mashed potato or some warmed greens.

SERVES 2

- 1 whole rainbow trout (350–400 g), cleaned, scaled and gutted (see Note)
- 3–4 tablespoons extra-virgin olive oil
- 1 lemon, sliced
- 1–2 day-old bread rolls, roughly chopped or torn
- 2 garlic cloves, finely chopped
- 155 g pitted kalamata olives
- bunch of flat-leaf parsley, leaves picked and chopped
- 50 g salted butter
- salt flakes and freshly ground black pepper

Preheat the oven to 180°C (conventional).

Rinse the rainbow trout and pat dry, inside and out, with paper towel.

In a baking tray, pour a 'lining' of good-quality extra virgin olive oil. Add the rainbow trout, then turn it over so it gets a good coating of oil and rub a little oil into its belly. Add 2–3 lemon slices and some of the bread, garlic, olives, parsley and a knob of butter into the cavity and season well. Arrange the rest of the filling ingredients around the baking tray – these will brown and create crunch and flavour pops that you will thank us for later!

Bake in the oven for around 30 minutes, or until the rainbow trout flesh goes a pale pink and firms a little and the skin browns.

To serve, transfer the rainbow trout to a platter with all the extras from the pan arranged on top (or take the baking tray to the table). The flesh will come away from the skin and bone very easily now that it is cooked. Using serving utensils, gently pull off the top fillet, lifting off the bone, then lift away the head and spine too – you may need to remove some of the bones here.

NOTE You could replace the rainbow trout with snapper for this recipe.

THE FISHMONGER'S SON

FISH PIE

We work with a pastry chef to create a fish pie that we sell frozen in our shop. This is our make-at-home version – a rustic take with chunky pieces of fish, carrot and potato. Fish pie is a lovely introduction to eating seafood.

SERVES 4–6

- 400 ml milk
- 100 ml white wine
- 100 ml dry sherry
- 100 ml fish stock (or water)
- 50 g salted butter
- 1 tablespoon extra-virgin olive oil
- 1 small brown onion, finely chopped
- 1 carrot, peeled and cut into 2 cm chunks
- 1 large potato, peeled and cut into 2 cm chunks
- 1–2 tablespoons plain flour
- 180 g salmon fillet, skin off, cut into 2 cm chunks
- 180 g rock ling fillet, skin off, cut into 2 cm chunks
- 100 g smoked salmon, cut into 2 cm chunks
- 180 g raw prawn cutlets, tails off, cut into 2 cm chunks
- handful of flat-leaf parsley leaves, chopped
- juice of 1 lemon
- 1 tablespoon finely chopped dill fronds, or to taste
- salt flakes and freshly ground black pepper
- 1 sheet puff pastry
- 1 egg, beaten, for egg wash

Preheat the oven to 200°C (conventional). Grease a 1.5–2 litre round ovenproof baking dish (25 × 5 cm) with butter.

Combine the milk, wine, sherry and stock in a jug and set aside.

Place the butter and olive oil in a deep non-stick frying pan on the stove and turn to medium heat. Once the butter has mostly melted, add the onion and cook for 1–2 minutes, then add the carrot and potato. Cook for 3–4 minutes, or until they begin to soften. Using a wooden spoon, stir in the flour until it dissolves, then add the liquid from the jug. Keep stirring slowly and steadily until it thickens, another 3–5 minutes.

Next, add the fish and prawns and cook for another 3–4 minutes, then stir in the parsley, lemon, dill and salt and pepper to taste. Remove from the heat to cool for around 10 minutes.

Transfer the filling to the baking dish and lay the puff pastry on top. Gently press the edges of the puff pastry onto the outer edge of the dish, covering the rim. Trim off any overhanging pastry. Use a sharp knife to make a cross incision in the centre of the pastry for the steam to escape, being careful not to push the centre of the pastry down onto the filling.

Brush with the egg wash and place in the oven to bake for 30 minutes, until the pastry is golden and crunchy.

We love to eat this just as is, scooped out into shallow bowls, but sometimes we add some peas on the side (or you can even add them to the pie if you want more veg).

NOTE You can add to and swap around the fish selection in this pie. As a rule, we always use one red fish, one white fish, one smoked fish and the prawns for texture, but you can sub in scallops for prawns or add mussels or clams.

ON THE STOVETOP

MASTER RECIPE

FOR FLOURED FRIED SEAFOOD

This master recipe is your go-to for flouring and frying seafood of all descriptions. Feel free to add in additional herbs, such as oregano or native pepper berry. Make it your own. We love to add lemon zest to ours.

Fish prepared this way is so satisfying as a light meal with a simple salad. You can also scale up this recipe as an appetiser to feed a crowd.

SERVES 4

- 200 g plain flour mixed with ⅔ teaspoon sea salt and ⅔ teaspoon freshly ground black pepper
- zest of 1 lemon
- olive oil for deep frying
- salt flakes, to serve
- lemon wedges, to serve
- good-quality aioli, to serve

CHOOSE FROM LIST BELOW (YOU WILL NEED 400 G IN TOTAL)

- 200 g fresh calamari hoods, including tentacles, cleaned
- 200 g raw prawns, peeled, deveined and butterflied, tails on
- 200 g white fish fillets (flathead, garfish, King George whiting, rock ling, etc.)
- 200 g local scallops

Place the seasoned flour in a deep bowl and mix in the lemon zest.

Heat the olive oil in a frying pan over medium–low heat. We rarely fry seafood on a high heat – always aim for medium–low heat for consistent results.

Flour the fish or shellfish using your hands.

Drop small batches of fish or shellfish into the oil – don't crowd the pan or it will cool the oil. The fish or shellfish needs to cook to a golden brown to ensure even cooking (see approximate cooking times below). The oil should be hot enough to get an instant sizzle but should not be smoking. If it's getting too hot, turn the temperature down. Once golden and cooked, remove the fish or shellfish with a slotted spoon and place on a plate lined with some paper towel to drain. Repeat until all of it is fried.

If the oil gets too 'floury,' empty the pan and add fresh oil – fresh oil gives you the best outcome.

Sprinkle the fried fish or shellfish with salt flakes and serve with lemon wedges and some good aioli.

COOKING TIMES

Calamari: 2–3 minutes; look for a light golden colour and watch it carefully as it firms up.

Prawns: 3–4 minutes; they will curl up tightly and turn pink – look for even colour.

White fish: 3–4 minutes, though thicker fish will take an extra 1–2 minutes; look for a light golden colour and bright white flesh.

Scallops: 2–3 minutes; look for a golden colour – they will firm up and should be tender when touched.

THE BEST FISH FOR CRUMBING

A delicate white fish will be pillowy soft when crumbed.

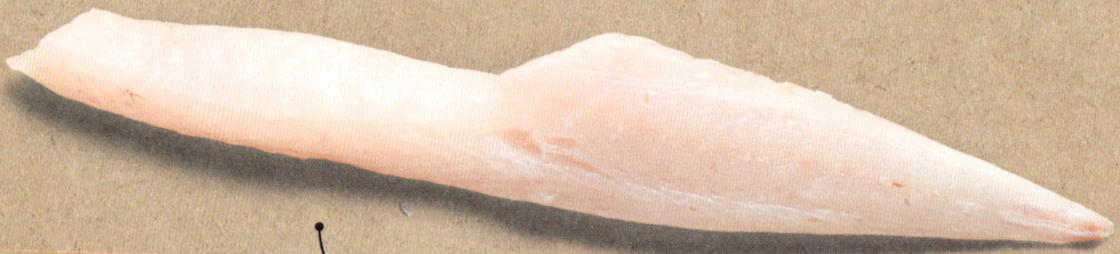

FLATHEAD TAILS

GARFISH

GUMMY SHARK (FLAKE)

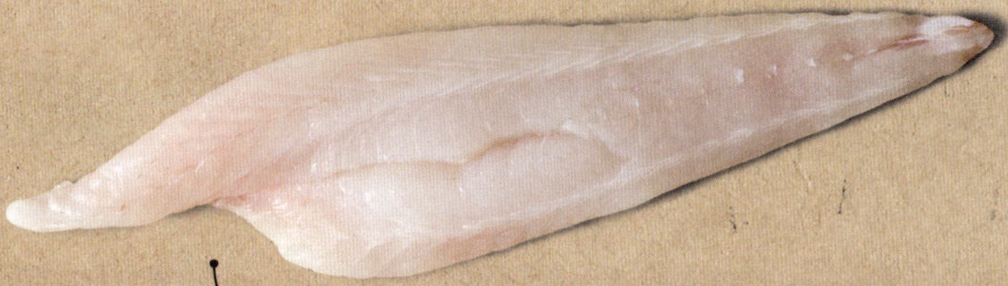

GURNARD

KING GEORGE WHITING

ROCK LING

MASTER RECIPE

FOR CRUMBED FISH

Panko or crumbed fish is one of the simplest ways to prepare fish and is widely loved by kids and adults alike. This recipe can be used for a large variety of seafood – from flathead, flake or rock ling to lovely, butterflied fillets like garfish or whiting. The crunchy crumb contrasts beautifully with the delicately cooked fish within. You can serve crumbed fish as it comes, or with a fresh salad. Either way, panko fish is delicious with mayo, so make sure you have some on the side!

SERVES 4

- 400 g fish fillets of your choice
- salt flakes
- freshly ground black pepper (optional)
- 150 g plain flour
- 180 g panko or coarse breadcrumbs (see Notes)
- bunch of flat-leaf parsley, leaves picked and chopped (optional – see Notes)
- olive oil for frying
- mayonnaise, to serve

Pat dry the fish fillets, lay them flat on a board and season with a little salt. If you're using a strongly flavoured or oily fish, you can add pepper here as well. Set the fish aside.

Place the flour in a deep bowl and whisk together with 250 ml (1 cup) of water – it should be just enough to create a light batter to dip the fillets into. The batter shouldn't be too watery and not as thick as fish-and-chip batter; all we are trying to achieve here is a preparatory base for the crumb.

In another deep bowl, add the breadcrumbs and parsley.

Dip a piece of fish into the flour and water mix, removing any excess on the side of the bowl, then transfer directly to the crumb mixture. Use your fingers to press the crumb gently onto the fish until it is well coated – when you lift it out of the bowl the crumbs should stay in place. Transfer to a separate plate and repeat with the rest of the fish.

Place the crumbed fillets in the fridge for at least 20 minutes before frying.

Preheat a non-stick frying pan with olive oil to a depth of 2 cm over medium heat. To test the oil, drop in a piece of the crumb – if it sizzles immediately you're good to go.

The aim is to fry the fillets until golden on both sides. A thinner fillet such as garfish will only take 1–2 minutes per side; something thicker like rock ling may take double the time. For crumbing, it's a good idea to choose fillets 1 cm thick or less – they will cook quickly and evenly. Don't let the oil smoke, and ensure you remove excess crumb or replace the oil if you're doing a big batch.

Serve with mayo and a light salad on the side.

NOTES We always make our own breadcrumbs and store them in an airtight container. It's the sort of thing you can do whenever you have leftover bread. Let your bread go stale for 1–2 days, pop it in the oven at 100°C (conventional) for around 5–10 minutes, just to take the moisture out, then pulse in a food processor. Don't pulverise the crumb – chop it just so it's a nice, chunky texture with some finer elements.

If preparing this crumbing mixture for children who are green averse, you can omit the parsley.

FLOURED FLATHEAD
&
PANZANELLA SALAD

Panzanella is the height of summer cooking, with simple, fresh flavours using produce when it's at its best. We often use gurnard for this dish, although it's not as readily available as flathead. Gurnard is very similar to flathead but a little milder.

SERVES 4

- 4 thick slices of ciabatta bread, roughly chopped (see Notes)
- 2 tablespoons extra-virgin olive oil
- salt flakes
- 3–4 firm good-quality tomatoes, chopped
- 1 shallot (red onion or white salad onion also work), finely sliced
- 12 flathead or gurnard fillets (600–700 g total), prepared as per the Master Recipe for Floured Fried Seafood on page 165
- handful of fresh basil leaves
- 2 teaspoons red wine vinegar
- 100 ml extra-virgin olive oil for dressing
- freshly ground black pepper

Preheat the oven to 150°C (conventional) and line a baking tray with baking paper.

Toss the bread pieces in a bowl with the olive oil to coat. Arrange the bread on the baking tray and season with a couple of pinches of salt. Bake in the oven for 10–15 minutes, or until crunchy and golden. Set aside to cool.

Arrange the tomato and shallot in a large bowl. Salt to taste at this stage to help the tomato release its juices – the juices add moisture to the bread when it is added later. Set aside.

Prepare the flathead as per the instructions on page 165 and cook it for 2–3 minutes on each side. It should cook reasonably quickly. The flesh should go from pink to white, and the exterior should be golden. Drain on a plate lined with paper towel.

Assemble the salad by adding the bread and basil leaves to the bowl with the tomato. Add the vinegar and olive oil and toss well to combine the flavours. Season to taste. The bread should get a little 'wet' with the juices from the tomato and the olive oil.

Divide the salad between four plates. There will be some leftover juices in the bottom of the bowl; spoon these over the salad. Place three flathead fillets on each plate and serve.

NOTES You can buy dried bread from the deli (we often keep this in the pantry – like our grandparents!).

Any in-season tomatoes will work well here, so feel free to mix them up.

You can also add cucumber or red or green capsicum to this salad.

PRAWN SAGANAKI

This Greek comfort food is wonderfully moreish and makes a quick midweek meal that you can scale up to serve a crowd. It is best accompanied with a good loaf of bread to mop up all the juices, although some steamed buttery rice is also a nice alternative, and how we ate this dish growing up.

SERVES 4

2 tablespoons extra-virgin olive oil
2 garlic cloves, finely chopped
1 teaspoon lemon zest
2 anchovy fillets, chopped
500 g cherry tomatoes
salt flakes and freshly ground black pepper
24 raw king prawns, shelled and deveined with tails on (see Note)
200 g Greek or Persian feta
small handful of flat-leaf parsley leaves, chopped, to serve
warm crusty bread, to serve

Preheat the oven to 200°C (conventional).

Heat a large, deep ovenproof pan over low heat then add the olive oil, garlic, lemon zest and anchovies. Cook gently, stirring, until the garlic is lightly golden and the anchovies have disintegrated. Add the cherry tomatoes and cook for 10–15 minutes, or until they have cooked down a little but are still chunky. Season to taste.

Add the prawns, stirring well to ensure they are coated with oil and tomato, then cook them until they start to turn pink and curl up, around 5 minutes. Remove from the heat.

Crumble the feta evenly over the top, then carefully transfer the hot pan to the oven to allow the feta to melt – this should only take a few minutes so keep an eye on it. The prawns will finish cooking through this process.

Remove the pan from the oven and sprinkle with parsley.

Transfer to a serving dish ready to plate into individual dishes at the table. Serve with fresh crusty bread to mop up all the goodness!

NOTE Shelled raw prawns are more flavoursome, but you can just as easily use raw prawn cutlets if you're wanting to speed up the preparation of this dish.

THE BEST FISH FOR FISH CAKES

Choose a flavourful but inexpensive fish or get tails, which are not so desirable – often these are cheaper, and once skinned they mince well.

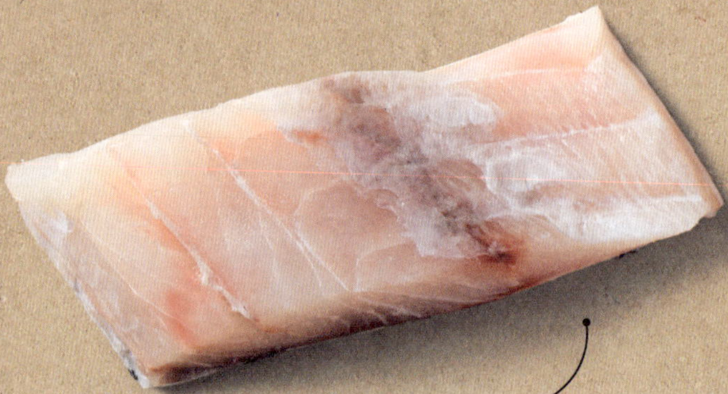

BARRAMUNDI

BLUE GRENADIER

SALMON

RED CURRY BARRAMUNDI

FISH CAKES

These red curry fish cakes were on high rotation in our store in the early days; they are super satisfying and filling. They also keep well in the fridge for a few days so are perfect to prep ahead of time.

MAKES 8

500 g potatoes
salt flakes and freshly ground black pepper
2 barramundi fillets (300 g total), skin on (see Note)
100 g Thai red curry paste
zest and juice of 1–2 limes
small bunch of coriander, leaves picked and finely chopped
300 g plain flour mixed with 1 teaspoon sea salt and 1 teaspoon freshly ground black pepper
3 eggs, beaten
300 g rustic breadcrumbs or panko crumbs
125 ml (½ cup) olive oil

Start by peeling, boiling and mashing the potatoes.

Preheat the oven to 180°C (conventional) and line a baking tray with baking paper.

Sprinkle some salt flakes and freshly ground black pepper onto the barramundi and place it skin-side down on the prepared tray. Place it in the oven to bake for approximately 30 minutes. It should be golden with bright white flesh when cut open.

Once it has cooled to the touch, remove the skin and flake the fish into a large bowl using your hands.

Add the cooled mashed potato, curry paste, lime zest and juice and coriander to the bowl with the fish and combine. Taste, then season with salt flakes and freshly ground black pepper. Spread the mix onto a shallow baking tray and leave to cool in the fridge for 20–30 minutes.

Once cooled, portion and shape the mixture into round patties, around 100 g each.

Place the seasoned flour, egg and breadcrumbs into three deep dishes, side by side.

Dip both sides of each patty in the flour, then egg, then breadcrumbs. Place them back into the fridge to firm up for 30 minutes.

Heat the olive oil in a frying pan on medium heat, then shallow fry the fish cakes for around 3–4 minutes on each side, until golden.

We make these as a snack or serve them with a side salad for a light meal. You can prepare the mixture 1–2 days ahead and crumb when ready to cook. These are best eaten warm but will keep in the fridge for 1–2 days.

NOTE You could just as easily use salmon for these fish cakes.

FRIED WHITEBAIT MARINATO

WITH A SQUEEZE OF LEMON

This appetiser is popular in our Greek and Italian homelands and it's great for a fry-up. When it comes to whitebait, the smaller the fish, the better, as whitebait is eaten whole. We love frying these up from fresh when we get them in the store, but frozen whitebait will work just as well.

SERVES 4 AS AN APPETISER

- 500 g whitebait (see Note)
- juice of 2 lemons, plus 1 lemon, halved, to serve
- 300 g plain flour mixed with 1 teaspoon sea salt and 1 teaspoon freshly ground black pepper
- 500 ml (2 cups) olive oil for deep frying
- salt flakes, to serve

Rinse and drain the whitebait in a colander, then transfer to a large bowl with the lemon juice and mix to ensure it's well coated. Set aside to marinate for around 15–20 minutes.

Drain the whitebait – we let it sit in a colander to dry off a bit.

Meanwhile, place the seasoned flour in a deep bowl. Dip the whitebait into the flour in small batches, making sure they are well coated.

Using a deep fryer or deep frying pan, heat the olive oil over medium heat until it sizzles when you drop a little flour in. Fry the whitebait in batches until they are golden brown and crunchy, around 2–3 minutes per batch. Remove with a slotted spoon and drain on paper towel.

Serve in a large shallow bowl with a sprinkle of salt flakes and some lemon halves for squeezing.

NOTE You can use school prawns in place of whitebait for this recipe.

RED EMPEROR

WITH WARMED GREENS

Our absolute favourite cooked green is cime di rapa, commonly known as rapini or broccoli rabe in Australia. Nonna Mariangela, God bless, cooked these beautifully. Dad di Florio has taken the lead on these in recent years in our family, and they are just divine with a piece of simply pan-fried fish. You could use a different fish, but we love red emperor when it's available as it has a firm, sweet texture in contrast to the bitterness of the greens.

SERVES 2

- 1 bunch of cime di rapa (rapini), cleaned and chopped (discard any thick stems)
- 2 teaspoons extra-virgin olive oil
- 3 garlic cloves, roughly chopped
- 75 g salted butter
- 400 g red emperor fillet or side, skin on and halved (see Note)
- 1 lemon, cut in half
- salt flakes and freshly ground black pepper

Set a pot of water on the stove to boil. Once boiling, salt the water and add the cime di rapa. Cook for 4–5 minutes, or until just tender. Drain and set aside, reserving 125 ml (½ cup) of the cooking water.

Place a non-stick frying pan on the stove, add the olive oil and garlic and bring to a gentle sizzle on medium–low heat before adding the drained cime di rapa and a little of the reserved cooking water. Cook for 3–4 minutes to warm through and imbue the rapa with the olive oil and garlic flavour. Set the cime di rapa aside until serving.

Warm another frying pan over medium heat and add the butter. Once the butter has melted, place the red emperor in the pan, skin-side down, for 4–5 minutes. Turn the fish and cook for another 2–3 minutes, then turn off the heat. Red emperor, when cooked, has a lovely firm white flesh, large flake and delicate flavour. Tip the pan and squeeze the lemon into the melted butter, then baste the fillets with the butter.

Divide the cime di rapa between two plates, spreading it out to make a bed for the fish. Place the red emperor fillet on the greens and be sure to drizzle with any lemony butter still in the pan. Season to taste.

NOTE You can easily sub in blue-eye or snapper for this dish.

FISH COTOLETTI

Every Italian kid we know grew up eating cotoletti. It's the ultimate comfort food – so much so, it's like a love language for mamas and nonnas. Laura's favourite meal is chicken cotoletti, and so it was inevitable that a fish version would find its way into our family repertoire. We often have cotoletti with warmed greens and oven-baked chips.

SERVES 4

- 12 flathead fillets (600–800 g total), skin off (see Note)
- salt flakes and freshly ground black pepper
- 3 eggs, beaten
- 100 g panko or homemade breadcrumbs (see Notes, page 168)
- 45 g pecorino, grated
- 2 tablespoons finely chopped flat-leaf parsley leaves
- olive oil for frying
- salt flakes, to serve

Lightly season the flathead fillets with salt flakes and freshly ground black pepper.

Place the egg in a deep bowl. In another bowl, combine the breadcrumbs, pecorino and parsley. Line a flat plate or baking tray with baking paper.

Dip the flathead in the egg, coating it completely, then into the breadcrumb bowl. Use your fingers to ensure the crumb coats all of the fish, then place it on the baking tray and repeat. Once you have crumbed all the fish, cover it with plastic wrap and transfer to the fridge for around 30 minutes.

Pour the olive oil into a frying pan to a depth of 2 cm and heat over medium–low. Once it is hot enough – you can test this by dropping in a little bit of crumb; if it sizzles it's ready – start cooking in small batches. Cook the flathead for 2–3 minutes each side until golden.

If the oil becomes too 'crumby', empty the pan and add fresh oil.

Transfer the fried flathead to a flat dish lined with paper towel to drain.

When all the flathead has been cooked, transfer it to a serving dish and sprinkle salt flakes on top.

NOTES This is a great base recipe – you can sub in all sorts of fish here, such as rock ling, swordfish and whiting.

Any leftover egg and crumbing mixture can be combined and shaped into small patties. Fry these with the flathead and serve as a delicious extra, straight from Laura's childhood!

BEER-BATTERED FISH

&

POTATO CAKES

Anthony's father, Kon, had a wholesale seafood business that serviced many fish and chip shops around Melbourne. Their flake was second to none! This simple, classic beer-battered dish is a nod to those businesses and those times, and one of Anthony's 'signature' dishes at home.

SERVES 4

6 fresh gummy shark (flake) fillets (600 g total) (see Note)
salt flakes
400 g plain flour
freshly ground black pepper
1 teaspoon baking powder
375 ml beer
zest of 1 lemon
olive oil or vegetable oil for deep frying
1 large potato
ketchup, to serve
mayo, to serve
lemon wedges, to serve (optional)

Start by lightly salting the fish and setting it aside in the fridge for 10 minutes. This will draw out any moisture and give you a better result.

In a shallow bowl, combine 100 g of the flour with a pinch each of salt flakes and freshly ground black pepper.

In a deep bowl, combine the remaining flour and the baking powder. Slowly pour in the beer, gently whisking as you go – you are aiming for a thin to medium texture. Whisk in the lemon zest. If the batter is too runny it will not stay on the fish, and if it's too thick the fish will not cook through. Set the batter aside for 10 minutes.

Prepare a pan for frying (we often use a wok) by pouring in the oil to a depth of 3–4 cm. Heat the oil on medium heat. While the oil is warming, remove the fish from the fridge and pat it dry with paper towel.

To test if the oil in the pan is hot enough, drop a little batter into the oil – it should sizzle when it's ready.

One at a time, hold a fillet by the corner and dip it in the flour to cover, then dunk it back and forth in the batter to coat. Use the edge of the bowl to gently remove any excess batter. Place the fillet immediately into the oil, then cook for 3–5 minutes until golden, turning over halfway through to ensure even colour and cooking. Don't overload the pan – cook one to two fillets at a time to maintain the oil temperature. Place on a plate lined with paper towel to drain.

Anthony usually serves his beer-battered fish with handmade potato cakes. He slices one large potato on the mandoline and prepares them in the same way as the fish. Fry for 3–5 minutes, turning once during cooking, until golden.

Good-quality ketchup and mayo are a must to serve with this classic dish, plus some lemon wedges if you like.

NOTE We always use flake, but you can very easily swap this out for flathead, rock ling, gurnard, or anything else your fishmonger recommends.

SIMPLE NIÇOISE SALAD
WITH FRESHLY SEARED TUNA

We tend to approach this dish like a deconstructed salad, building up a layer of delicious morsels and drizzling a tasty dressing on top. This salad is great for lunch, when you want something filling but don't want to do much cooking. We *always* use seared fresh tuna, not canned, for niçoise salad.

SERVES 4

olive oil for cooking
1 tuna loin fillet (350 g)
salt flakes and freshly ground black pepper
1 head baby gem lettuce, leaves washed and separated
4 soft-boiled eggs, halved
8 baby potatoes, boiled in salted water and chopped in half
250 g green beans, topped, tailed and blanched
3 tomatoes, quartered
3 tablespoons chopped flat-leaf parsley leaves
handful of pitted black olives

DRESSING
3–4 tablespoons extra-virgin olive oil
50 ml red wine vinegar or juice of 1 lemon
1 tablespoon wholegrain mustard
salt flakes and freshly ground black pepper

Start by preparing the dressing. In a jar, add extra-virgin olive oil, red wine vinegar, mustard and salt and pepper to taste. Put the lid on the jar, shake it up and set aside.

Heat a little olive oil in a non-stick griddle pan over medium heat and cook the tuna. If you like it rare, just sear it for 1–2 minutes on each side. We prefer to cook it through to medium for this dish, so we leave it on for another for 1–2 minutes. Add salt and pepper, to taste, and set aside.

Arrange the lettuce leaves on a large serving plate, then start layering the other elements – boiled eggs, potatoes, green beans, tomatoes, parsley and olives.

Cut the tuna into rough chunks and arrange the pieces through the salad. Drizzle the dressing over the top and toss very gently. This is a complete meal and perfect for a quick Sunday lunch.

SWORDFISH WITH BURNT BUTTER

CAPER SAUCE & POTATO SALAD

Capers and lemon are heaven sent for so many types of seafood, particularly swordfish. This dish evolved out of a desire for something a little different from the standard pan-fried fish with salad and veggies. We love this quick dish with a side of potato salad, but you could serve it with mash and some warmed greens if you prefer.

SERVES 2

- salt flakes and freshly ground black pepper
- 2 swordfish steaks (400 g total) (see Note)
- 1 tablespoon extra-virgin olive oil
- 150 g salted butter (we prefer cultured butter for this)
- 2 tablespoons salted capers, rinsed and chopped
- juice of 1 lemon

POTATO SALAD

- 1 tablespoon mayonnaise
- 1 tablespoon crème fraîche or plain yoghurt
- 1 tablespoon salted capers, rinsed and chopped
- zest and juice of ½ lemon
- 1 tablespoon chopped dill fronds
- 1 teaspoon extra-virgin olive oil
- ¼ red onion, finely chopped
- 8 baby potatoes, boiled and cut in half
- salt flakes and freshly ground black pepper

For the potato salad, combine the mayo, crème fraîche or yoghurt, capers, lemon zest, dill, olive oil and onion in a bowl. Add the cooled potatoes and lemon juice. Taste and season as required.

Very lightly season the swordfish steaks.

Warm a griddle pan – a regular frying pan will also work fine – over medium heat. Add the olive oil and allow it to warm a little, then add the swordfish.

Cooking a piece of swordfish is like cooking chicken or steak: allow it to colour and watch the progression as it begins to cook through to a bright white, around 3–4 minutes depending on the thickness. Add the butter and capers to the pan, turn the swordfish over and cook for another 2–3 minutes. Add a squeeze of lemon juice to the pan. The butter will brown during this process – tip the pan and baste the swordfish with the butter.

Remove the swordfish from the pan and plate up, evenly distributing the burnt butter caper sauce over each piece. Serve with the potato salad on the side.

NOTE You could sub in tuna or marlin instead of swordfish here.

TERIYAKI SEAFOOD SKEWERS

WITH SALMON, ROCK LING & PRAWNS

Seafood skewers are a great way to showcase a few different types of seafood. We like to have three types of seafood on the skewer and cook them on a griddle pan for a quick dinner (or on the flat plate of the barbecue). Salmon also works really well on its own, if you prefer.

MAKES 6 SKEWERS

6 short bamboo skewers
200 g salmon, cut into 2 cm cubes
200 g rock ling, cut into 2 cm cubes
6 raw prawn cutlets, cleaned and deveined, tails on
1 white onion, quartered, layers broken up
vegetable oil for brushing
steamed rice, to serve
wasabi, to serve
sesame seeds for sprinkling

TERIYAKI MARINADE

3 tablespoons soy sauce
3 tablespoons brown sugar
1 garlic clove, grated
1 teaspoon grated ginger

Start by soaking the skewers in a bowl of water for at least 30 minutes (this prevents them from burning). You can just as easily use metal skewers if you have them.

Make the marinade by combining the soy, brown sugar, garlic, ginger and 1 tablespoon of water in a small bowl. Pour this over the fish and seafood and leave to marinate for 15–30 minutes in the fridge.

Place a griddle plan over medium heat (or heat a barbecue flat plate to medium).

Thread one piece of each fish/seafood onto the skewers with some onion in between.

Brush vegetable oil onto the fish skewers and place them on the griddle pan or barbecue flat plate. Baste the skewers with any leftover marinade while they are cooking. Cook for 2–3 minutes, then turn the skewers and brush again with marinade. Keep turning and brushing with marinade to get a good colour all over, for a total cooking time of around 8 minutes.

Serve with steamed rice mixed through with a little wasabi and sprinkled with sesame seeds.

THE BEST FISH FOR SOUP

Fish soup is delicate and does not take long to prepare. Choose something light that lends itself to the process.

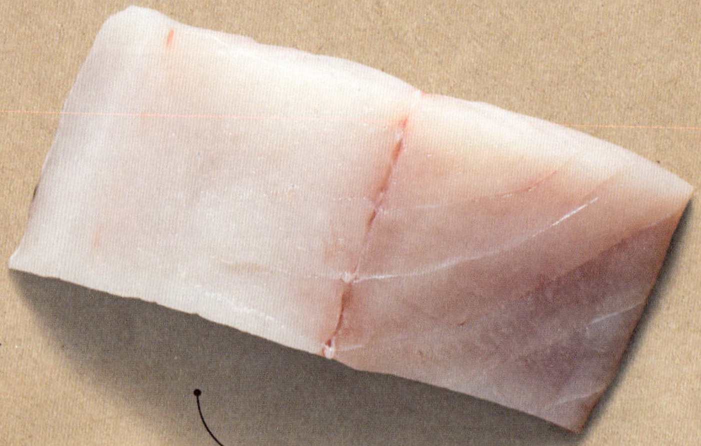

BLUE-EYE

SNAPPER

AVGOLEMONO FISH SOUP

Anthony grew up eating this classic Greek soup, which is a sublime combination of rice in an eggy-lemony broth. We love making this soup for our little family in the winter months, with the fish and vegetables cooked in the broth served on the side.

SERVES 4

- 2 large potatoes, peeled and quartered
- 2 carrots, peeled and chopped
- 1 celery stalk, chopped
- small bunch of flat-leaf parsley
- 1 whole snapper (1–1.5 kg), scaled, gutted and chopped into 3 or 4 cutlets
- extra-virgin olive oil, to serve
- 2 cups white rice
- 2 eggs, beaten
- juice of 2 small lemons

Place the vegetables and parsley in a large, deep pot with 2 litres of water and cook on medium heat for around 10 minutes, or until they start to soften. Place the snapper carefully on top of the vegetables and continue to cook for another 20 minutes, until the fish has cooked through and the flesh easily comes away from the bone.

Carefully remove the fish, potatoes, carrots and celery using a slotted spoon and place on a platter to serve, keeping warm. We like to remove the fish flesh from the bones and arrange it on the plate with the potatoes and carrots, and add a drizzle of olive oil before serving.

Strain the remaining stock into another container through a sieve, then return to the pot and cook over medium–low heat. Add the rice, stirring regularly. Once the rice has cooked al dente, take the pot off the heat and let it sit for a few minutes.

Add the egg and lemon juice to a jug and stir well to combine.

Start stirring the soup slowly and continuously – do not stop – and gently pour the lemon mix into the soup. The soup should start to become a milky white colour. It's important to stir continuously otherwise the eggs will scramble. This creates the classic avgolemono flavour.

Serve the soup in bowls and enjoy with the fish and vegetables on the side. You can add pieces of the snapper back into the soup if you like – or eat as you like.

SEAFOOD YOUVETSI

We adore this fragrant, hearty one-pot winter stew! It's our seafood version of the classic Greek staple, youvetsi. We use a cast-iron Dutch oven on the stovetop to make this dish, which lends itself to the rustic feel – but we've also improvised while on holidays and used a wok with a lid and it worked very well.

SERVES 4

- 1 tablespoon extra-virgin olive oil, plus extra for drizzling
- 3 garlic cloves, finely chopped
- 250 ml (1 cup) white wine
- 500 g tomato passata
- 500 ml (2 cups) fish stock
- 300 g risoni (orzo) pasta
- 500 g marinara mix (salmon, rock ling, prawn cutlets, vongole)
- salt flakes and freshly ground black pepper
- zest of 1 lemon
- handful of flat-leaf parsley leaves, finely chopped
- chilli oil, to serve (optional)

Start with a cold Dutch oven coated well with olive oil. Turn the heat to medium–low and add the garlic. Gently sauté the garlic until it is fragrant, then add the wine and allow the alcohol to cook off. Add the passata, stock and around 750 ml of water to create a very loose sauce. Bring the sauce to a gentle boil.

Once boiling, add the risoni and allow it to cook, stirring occasionally, until almost al dente as per the packet instructions.

When the risoni is almost al dente, add the seafood. It will only take about 4–5 minutes to cook. As soon as the vongole open, take the pan off the heat.

Season to taste with salt flakes and freshly ground black pepper, add the lemon zest and stir through.

Serve in bowls with a sprinkle of parsley on top. Add a drizzle of extra-virgin olive oil and some chilli oil (if using).

CRUMBED SARDINE FILLETS WITH MIXED LEAVES

Sardines have a unique, full-bodied flavour for such a tiny fish. Some people never grow into them and others just can't get enough of them – fried, on toast, in pasta … Sardines are packed with nutrients and really are very good for you. This is a cracking working-from-home lunch, as you can have these crumbed and ready in the fridge.

SERVES 2

- 6 sardine fillets
- salt flakes and freshly ground black pepper
- 3 tablespoons finely chopped flat-leaf parsley leaves
- 240 g rustic breadcrumbs
- 300 g plain flour
- 250 ml cold water
- 1 tablespoon extra-virgin olive oil
- 2 teaspoons white balsamic vinegar (or whichever vinegar you prefer)
- 120 g mixed salad leaves, washed
- 3–4 tablespoons olive oil for frying
- 1 lemon, halved
- chilli oil, to serve (optional)

Lay your sardine fillets out and lightly season the flesh with salt and black pepper, then set aside for 10 minutes.

Prepare two deep bowls. Combine the parsley and breadcrumbs in the first bowl. In the second bowl, add the flour and cold water, gently whisking to combine.

Holding a fillet at one end, dip it in the flour and water mixture, making sure it is thoroughly coated. Place straight into the crumb mixture, using your fingers to ensure an even coating. Repeat with all the fillets.

Place the fillets in the fridge for 5–10 minutes to firm up.

Combine the extra-virgin olive oil, vinegar and salt and pepper, to taste. Dress the leaves, then arrange on the side of a serving plate.

Heat the olive oil in a frying pan over medium heat. Pan-fry the sardine fillets for around 2 minutes on each side, until the crumb is golden and crunchy. Drain on paper towel.

Arrange the sardine fillets next to the salad leaves and add a squeeze of lemon or a drizzle of chilli oil, if using.

NOTE You can crumb and prep your sardines the day before as they will keep well in the fridge.

PRAWN & CHORIZO SALAD

WITH TOMATO

This filling and flavourful salad goes well with a barbecue spread, or makes a complete meal with a side of toasted bread for mopping up the juices. The oil from the chorizo is a wonderful vehicle to cook the prawns. It's a super simple meal that showcases great produce – perfect for summer dining!

SERVES 4

- 4 chorizo sausages (400 g), sliced diagonally
- 350 g raw prawn cutlets, tails on
- 5 firm tomatoes, chopped
- 1 small red onion, finely sliced
- 1 tablespoon sherry vinegar (or red wine vinegar)
- 2 tablespoons extra-virgin olive oil
- salt flakes and freshly ground black pepper
- small handful of flat-leaf parsley leaves

Preheat a frying pan over medium heat.

Place the chorizo slices in the hot pan and cook for around 5–8 minutes, until browned and they have released all their oil. Remove with a slotted spoon and set aside in your serving dish.

Add the prawn cutlets to the chorizo oil and cook – turning to ensure even cooking – for 3–4 minutes, until pink and tightly curled. Remove with a spoon and add to the serving dish with the chorizo.

Add the tomato and onion to the serving dish and gently toss through with the prawn and chorizo. Dress with the vinegar and extra-virgin olive oil, and season with salt and pepper to taste. Sprinkle the parsley leaves over the top and serve.

SWORDFISH STIR-FRY

WITH NOODLES

We love Asian cuisine in our home, so we often make a quick and tasty stir-fry. Using swordfish is a game-changer – texturally, it's like meat, and handles just as well through the cooking process.

You can change up the vegetables here to whatever is in season or any particular family favourites.

SERVES 4

- 1 tablespoon vegetable oil
- 1 teaspoon grated ginger
- 2 portions swordfish (400 g total), cut into 2 cm cubes
- 1 teaspoon raw sugar
- 1 tablespoon Shaoxing wine
- 1 brown onion, chopped
- 200 g snow peas, topped and tailed
- 1 large carrot, sliced diagonally
- 275 ml oyster sauce
- 400 g pre-cooked egg noodles
- sesame oil for drizzling

Heat a wok to medium–high heat and add the vegetable oil and ginger. Toss briefly, just until aromatic.

Add the swordfish and keep it moving so it doesn't stick. Keep tossing until it starts to colour. Sprinkle in the sugar and let it melt away, then pour in the Shaoxing and let it evaporate a little.

Use a slotted spoon to take the swordfish out just before it's cooked, around 4 minutes, and set aside.

Add the vegetables now and toss until they gently soften – ensure they still have a bit of crunch. Return the swordfish to the wok and add the oyster sauce. Cook for another minute or so, then add the noodles and gently stir through until everything is well coated.

Turn off the heat and drizzle a little sesame oil over the top. It's ready to serve straight from the wok.

FISH NUGGETS

FOR THE YOUNG AT HEART

These fish nuggets are squarely aimed at the little ones – or those who are young at heart. You can use the crumbing technique in this recipe for many different types of fish, so it's a good one to have in your repertoire.

MAKES 12

- 500 g mid- to tail-end pieces of rock ling or similar firm, white fish (see Note)
- salt flakes and freshly ground black pepper
- 150 g plain flour
- 200 g panko breadcrumbs
- zest of 1 lemon
- olive oil for frying
- aioli or ketchup, to serve

Cut the fish into bite-size pieces, season with a sprinkling of salt flakes and freshly ground black pepper and set aside.

Place the flour in a deep bowl and whisk together with 250 ml (1 cup) of water – it should be just enough to create a light batter to dip the fillets into. It shouldn't be too watery and not as thick as a fish-and-chip batter; all we are trying to achieve here is a preparatory base for the crumbed nuggets.

In another deep bowl, combine the breadcrumbs and lemon zest. Line a flat plate or baking tray with baking paper.

Dip and coat each piece of fish in the batter, then into the crumb to coat. Place the crumbed fish on the baking tray and repeat until all the nuggets are crumbed. Place in the fridge to firm up for around 20–30 minutes.

Pour the olive oil into a frying pan to a depth of 2 cm and heat over medium heat. To test if the oil in the pan is hot enough, drop a little batter into the oil – it should sizzle when it's ready. Add the fish nuggets and cook for 3–5 minutes, turning, until golden.

Serve with aioli, ketchup, or whatever your little people like best.

NOTE Swordfish, gummy shark (flake) or marlin would work a treat here too.

THE BEST SEAFOOD FOR CURRY

Choose firm-fleshed fish that will hold its shape and not break apart over the cooking time.

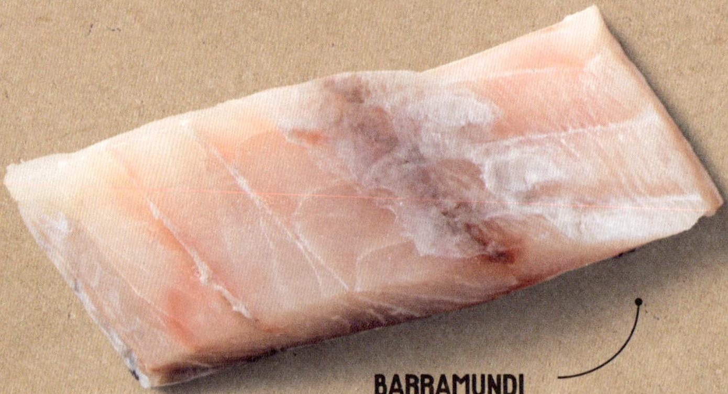

BARRAMUNDI

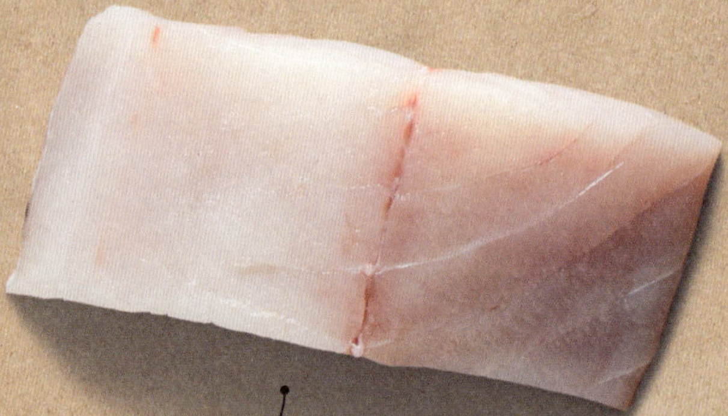

BLUE-EYE

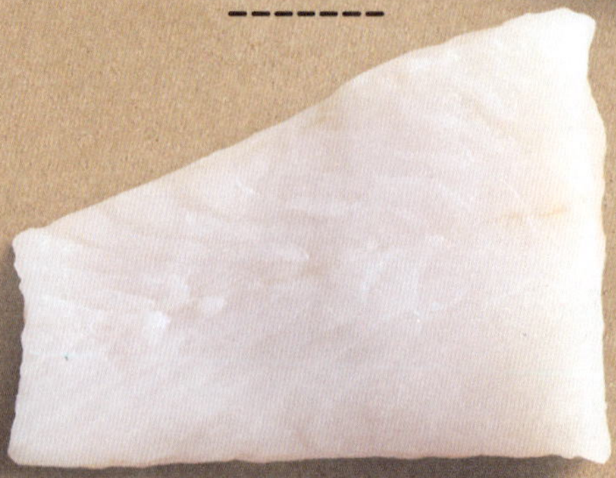

MONKFISH

PRAWNS
ROCK LING
SNAPPER
SWORDFISH

THAI-STYLE FISH CURRY

Once you nail an easy fish curry like this it becomes a rewarding and hearty staple. We are often time-poor, so we always keep a good-quality curry base and a can of coconut milk in the pantry to whip up this curry on a whim.

In our store, the most popular fish we sell for curries is rock ling or monkfish.

SERVES 4

- 2 tablespoons vegetable oil
- 100 g good-quality Thai red curry paste
- 400 ml can coconut milk
- 3 dried makrut lime leaves
- 2 dried red chillies (optional – if you like extra heat)
- 1 brown onion, chopped
- 1 zucchini (or pumpkin), chopped
- 125 g green beans, chopped
- 250 g bamboo shoots
- 2 rock ling fillets (500 g total), skin off and cubed (see Note)
- steamed jasmine rice, to serve
- coriander leaves, to serve (optional)
- fried shallots, to serve (optional)

In a wok, heat the vegetable oil over medium heat and fry off the curry paste for a minute or so until all the fragrances are released.

Add the coconut milk, makrut lime leaves and the dried chilli (if using) and bring it to a gentle simmer.

Next, add in the veggies and allow them to cook for around 5 minutes, or until just tender. You may need to add up to 125 ml (½ cup) of water here if you need extra liquid.

Last, add the fish and cook for just 1–2 minutes, then turn off the heat and cover the wok with a lid. Let the fish finish cooking in the residual heat for another 3–5 minutes, stirring gently once or twice. Ling does not take long, so keep an eye on it – overcooked ling can be tough. You want it to be pillowy soft.

Line four bowls with steamed rice and spoon the curry generously on the top ... enjoy! You can serve with some coriander leaves or fried shallots if you like.

NOTE Other beautiful fish to use for this curry include barramundi, swordfish and blue-eye, or even prawns.

MUSSELS IN RED WINE SAUCE

When Anthony was growing up in Dromana, one of the local fishermen would sell fresh mussels from his front yard. Anthony's mum would buy them regularly, especially over the summer months.

Make sure you buy some beautiful crusty bread for this dish, to soak up the delicious juices.

SERVES 2

1 small brown onion, chopped
3 garlic cloves, finely chopped
1 bay leaf
2 tablespoons extra-virgin olive oil
300 g tomato passata
1 kg mussels, scrubbed
150 ml red wine
salt flakes and freshly ground black pepper
baguette, to serve

In a large pot or wok on medium heat, sauté the onion, garlic and bay leaf in olive oil for 2–3 minutes or until the garlic is fragrant and the onion is tender.

Add the tomato passata and bring to a gentle boil. Allow the sauce to cook down for around 10 minutes, then add the mussels and wine.

Cover with a lid and simmer for another 10 minutes, or until the shells have opened.

Once the mussels have opened, remove them with a slotted spoon and divide between two bowls.

Turn up the heat and stir continuously to reduce the sauce and make it a little thicker; this should take another 3–5 minutes. Taste, then season with salt flakes and freshly ground black pepper. Discard the bay leaf.

Pour the sauce over the mussels and serve with crusty baguette.

CONVERSION CHARTS

Measuring cups and spoons may vary slightly from one country to another, but the difference is generally not enough to affect a recipe. All cup and spoon measures are level.

One Australian metric measuring cup holds 250 ml (8 fl oz), one Australian metric tablespoon holds 20 ml (4 teaspoons) and one Australian metric teaspoon holds 5 ml. North America, New Zealand and the UK use a 15 ml (3-teaspoon) tablespoon.

LENGTH

METRIC	IMPERIAL
3 mm	⅛ inch
6 mm	¼ inch
1 cm	½ inch
2.5 cm	1 inch
5 cm	2 inches
18 cm	7 inches
20 cm	8 inches
23 cm	9 inches
25 cm	10 inches
30 cm	12 inches

LIQUID MEASURES

One American pint = 500 ml (17 fl oz)
One Imperial pint = 600 ml (20 fl oz)

CUP	METRIC	IMPERIAL
⅛ cup	30 ml	1 fl oz
¼ cup	60 ml	2 fl oz
⅓ cup	80 ml	2½ fl oz
½ cup	125 ml	4 fl oz
⅔ cup	160 ml	5 fl oz
¾ cup	180 ml	6 fl oz
1 cup	250 ml	8 fl oz
2 cups	500 ml	16 fl oz
2¼ cups	560 ml	20 fl oz
4 cups	1 litre	34 fl oz

DRY MEASURES

The most accurate way to measure dry ingredients is to weigh them. However, if using a cup, add the ingredient loosely to the cup and level with a knife; don't compact the ingredient unless the recipe requests 'firmly packed'.

METRIC	IMPERIAL
15 g	½ oz
30 g	1 oz
60 g	2 oz
125 g	4 oz (¼ lb)
185 g	6 oz
250 g	8 oz (½ lb)
375 g	12 oz (¾ lb)
500 g	16 oz (1 lb)
1 kg	32 oz (2 lb)

OVEN TEMPERATURES

CELSIUS	FAHRENHEIT
100°C	200°F
120°C	250°F
150°C	300°F
160°C	325°F
180°C	350°F
200°C	400°F
220°C	425°F

CELSIUS	GAS MARK
110°C	¼
130°C	½
140°C	1
150°C	2
170°C	3
180°C	4
190°C	5
200°C	6
220°C	7
230°C	8
240°C	9
250°C	10

ACKNOWLEDGEMENTS

Seafood is a big part of our everyday lives and celebrations. Writing this book and sharing our family recipes has been an experience that has filled us with all the feels and memories as we revisited family treasures and created new food stories. We hope it awakens in you some ideas for cooking with seafood at home.

*

Our thanks to all the team at Plum for being so professional, kind and accommodating. This experience has exceeded all of our expectations!

A very special thank you to Mary Small, our publisher, for this wonderful opportunity. Writing this book has been the realisation of a dream for us. Your beautiful energy and excitement for the project has propelled us forward and lifted us up. The world, publishing and otherwise, is so much the better with you in it. Thank you for believing in our seafood vision and taking us on this incredible journey, we feel so thankful and inspired.

Clare Marshall, our project editor, thank you for your beautiful kind way, enthusiasm, patience and gentle nudges. We got there!

Martine Lleonart, our editor, thank you for organising our jumble of words into something everyone can understand, not just us.

Michelle Mackintosh, our designer, thank you for this incredible book design that reflects the vibe that is The Fishmonger's Son.

Sarah Watson, our photoshoot chef, thank you for making our recipes come to life and helping us iron out the kinks. What a joy it was to share the kitchen with you, Meryl Batlle, Gemma Smith and Jonte Carlson. You're all such incredible chefs and you made us feel so comfortable.

Lee Blaylock, our stylist, what an incredible eye and energy you have. You made our food look so delicious and so 'us' and were such fun to work with.

Mark Roper, our photographer, thank you for your wonderful eye for detail and your humour. You and Lee are certainly a dream team.

Shooting this book was the most fulfilling experience and we owe that to every one of our shoot team. Thank you for your care, humour and for being complete legends at what you do. We have been so honoured to work on this project with you.

Thank you to Shirow Murakashi, our sushi chef and very special part of The Fishmonger's Son family. We are so grateful to you, Shirow, for your energy, skill and enthusiasm.

To our beautiful clients, many of whom we now consider friends, thank you for taking us into the Carlton North community, sharing your stories and recipes, and trusting in us.

Thanks to our parents, brothers, sisters, nieces, nephews, special cousins and mates for being our biggest cheerleaders and collaborators. For mucking in with us on this wild ride, with fish, renovations, childcare, lending an ear, advice, sharing a recipe and reminding us to keep going and enjoy the process. There is nothing that makes us happier than sitting around the table with you, eating, laughing, drinking and sharing stories. You guys hold us up, we love you and are so proud of our Greek and Italian heritage.

Kosti and Olympia, you two are our heart and soul. We hope you are proud of Daddy and Mamma.

And lastly to you, the reader. Thank you for coming along on this journey. We hope you enjoy this book and it gives you a little more confidence with seafood at home.

A&LX

INDEX

SMOOTH
SEAS
DON'T
MAKE
SKILLED
SAILORS
ONLY
DEAD
FISH
GO
WITH THE
FLOW

D

E

F

G

Q

R

S

T

V

W

Y

Z

Pan Macmillan acknowledges the Traditional Custodians of Country throughout Australia and their connections to lands, waters and communities. We pay our respect to Elders past and present and extend that respect to all Aboriginal and Torres Strait Islander peoples today. We honour more than sixty thousand years of storytelling, art and culture.

A Plum book

First published in 2024 by
Pan Macmillan Australia Pty Limited
Level 25, 1 Market Street,
Sydney, NSW 2000, Australia

Level 3, 112 Wellington Parade,
East Melbourne, VIC 3002, Australia

Designed by Michelle Mackintosh
Typeset by Megan Ellis
Edited by Martine Lleonart
Index by Helena Holmgren
Photography by Mark Roper
Food and prop styling by Lee Blaylock
Food preparation by Meryl Batlle, Jonte Carlson, Gemma Smith and Sarah Watson
Colour reproduction by Splitting Image Colour Studio
Printed and bound in China by Hang Tai Printing Co. Ltd.

A CIP catalogue record for this book is available from the National Library of Australia.

10 9 8 7 6 5 4 3 2 1